HIGH PERFORMANCE
BENCHMARKING

OTHER McGRAW-HILL BOOKS BY
H. JAMES HARRINGTON

HIGH PERFORMANCE BENCHMARKING

20 Steps to Success

H. James Harrington
Principal, Ernst & Young LLP

James S. Harrington
Journalist, Gavilan Newspapers

McGraw-Hill

New York   San Francisco   Washington, D.C.   Auckland   Bogotá
Caracas   Lisbon   London   Madrid   Mexico City   Milan
Montreal   New Delhi   San Juan   Singapore
Sydney   Tokyo   Toronto

Library of Congress Cataloging-in-Publication Data

Harrington, H. J. (H. James)
    High performance benchmarking : 20 steps to success / H. James
Harrington, James S. Harrington.
        p.   cm.
    Includes index.
    ISBN 0-07-026774-X (alk. paper)
    1. Benchmarking (Management)   I. Harrington, James S.   II. Title.
HD62.15.H3696   1995
658.5'62—dc20   95-20734
                                                          CIP

McGraw-Hill

A Division of The McGraw-Hill Companies

1 2 3 4 5 6 7 8 9 0   QBP/QBP   9 0 0 9 8 7 6 5

ISBN 0-07-026774-X

*The sponsoring editor for this book was Philip Ruppel, the editing
supervisor was David E. Fogarty, and the production supervisor was
Donald Schmidt. It was set in Fairfield by Victoria Khavkina of
McGraw-Hill's Professional Book Group composition unit.*

Printed and bound by Quebecor-Book Press

McGraw-Hill books are available at special quantity discounts to use
as premiums and sales promotions, or for use in corporate training
programs. For more information, please write to the Director of
Special Sales, McGraw-Hill, 11 West 19th Street, New York, NY
10011. Or contact your local bookstore.

 This book is printed on recycled, acid-free paper containing
a minimum of 50% recycled de-inked fiber.

My father asked me to write the dedication for this book. He made a few suggestions such as dedicating it to my friends, wife, or mom. But really there is only one choice.

This book is dedicated to you, dad. I love you.
                                    James S. Harrington

CONTENTS

PREFACE

For the first time, all the benchmarking applications are brought together in one book that covers competitive product testing, reverse engineering, competitive analysis, competitive shopping, and process benchmarking. Combining these very different approaches to benchmarking processes, products, and services provides an organization with a decided competitive advantage.

No matter how good your organization is, or how well regarded your products and/or services are, you cannot stop improving. You cannot stand still. When you do, you really are not standing still; you are slipping backward, because your competition is constantly improving.

One of the best ways to keep improving your organization is to benchmark. Benchmarking is a systematic way to identify superior products, services, processes, and practices that can be adopted by or adapted to your organization to reduce costs, decrease cycle times, increase reliability, cut inventories, and provide greater satisfaction to your customers. *High Performance Benchmarking* provides specific information, suggestions, guidelines, and checklists to help you start, maintain, and wrap up a benchmarking project.

H. James Harrington started benchmarking the benchmarking process in the late 1960s, and this database has expanded rapidly. In the last 10 years, process benchmarking has become the "in" thing to do. This book is built upon over 30 years of personal benchmarking experiences, successful and unsuccessful, and the many books and articles written on the subject during this period. It also takes into consideration award-winning benchmarking organizational approaches.

In preparing this book, we turned the tables on the benchmarking process and applied it to itself, thereby defining the world-class benchmarking processes. After careful study, we then designed a new benchmarking process that incorporates the best features of each of the many world-class approaches being used today. The result, we believe, in terms of actual performance, is the best of breed.

If this is your first benchmarking experience, prepare for some major surprises. In contrast to continuous improvement gains of 10 to 20 percent a year, benchmarking can result in improvements as great as 2000 percent in as short as 8 months. The average benchmarking process will reduce cost, cycle time, and error rates by 20 to 60 percent. If you don't believe us, just ask Xerox, IBM, Federal Express, and Ford Motor Company. They are all believers in, and users of, the benchmarking process.

Ernst & Young LLP and the American Quality Foundation conducted an extensive international quality study that found a statistical correlation between benchmarking and organizational performance (profit, productivity, and quality). Benchmarking is one of the few management practices that can be statistically validated as being a key driver for improvement in the best organizations.

Books like *Business Process Improvement*, by H. James Harrington and *Benchmarking*, by Robert Camp, tell you about the process. However, these popular books focus only on one leg of the three-legged stool that makes up benchmarking.

- Processes—business process benchmarking
- Services—competitive shopping benchmarking

- Products—reverse engineering/competitive product testing benchmarking

To date, the books that have been written are directed at business processes and have completely missed two-thirds of the benchmarking activity. There are four distinctly different benchmarking classifications that every organization must consider. They are:

- Business processes
- Equipment
- Manufacturing (production) processes
- Products and services

High Performance Benchmarking is the first book to provide a complete understanding of how to manage the total benchmarking process in any organization in order to maximize results. If you plan on incorporating a benchmarking process within your organization, we recommend that you use the detailed task-by-task benchmarking implementation manual entitled *The Complete Benchmarking Implementation Guide*, published by McGraw-Hill, in conjunction with the interactive computer-assisted learning program entitled *Benchmarking with H. James Harrington*, produced by LearnerFirst, Inc. of Birmingham, Alabama.

Everyone agrees that benchmarking is hard work. Now you have a guide that will greatly simplify the total process. With this guide as a tool, the benchmarking process will not run you; you will run it.

H. James Harrington
James S. Harrington

ACKNOWLEDGMENTS

I want to acknowledge the many contributions to this book made by the team at Ernst & Young LLP. The book reflects not only our personal experiences but also the experience and input from many of Ernst & Young's consultants.

My gratitude is extended to Debi Guido, who converted and edited endless hours of dictation into the finished product, and to Terry Ozan, for his support on this project and his leadership.

I would also like to recognize the fine work done by Edith Boisvert of J. C. Savard Consultants and Michael Martel of SystemCorp in preparing the figures used throughout this book.

Finally, I would be remiss in not acknowledging the efforts put in by my sweet Marguerite (my wife). She was always there with a kind word of encouragement when things got overbearing, and her work in proofing and standardizing the book's format was very valuable.

H. James Harrington

INTRODUCTION TO BENCHMARKING

BECOMING BETTER THAN THE BEST

With the intense competition in industry today, simply meeting or beating past performance will not result in the level of improvement necessary to remain competitive. Organizations must achieve quantum improvements in productivity, quality, reliability, and responsiveness to drive down costs and keep customers/consumers delighted.

We are all in an automobile race of sorts, but most organizational drivers don't know, and many don't care about, where they are positioned on the track. They look around and see a competitor in the race car behind them and take comfort in believing they are in the lead, not realizing the competitor is about to lap them. If the organization's pit crew (employees) gets the word to the driver (management) that the organization is behind, what action should the driver take? Should the organization do one or more of the following?

- Standardize processes
- Retrench
- Develop new systems
- Buy new technology
- Centralize
- Decentralize
- Reengineer processes
- Redesign processes
- Set up service centers
- Downsize
- Train employees
- Outsource

- Replace the CEO
- Reorganize
- Use more information technology

- Change management
- Automate
- Declare Chapter 11 bankruptcy

The most common mistake organizations make is to do nothing. It is a mistake because it harms management's credibility and often impacts future competitiveness. But most managers have been burned in the past by some of the improvement activities that they have accepted on a blind leap of faith. As a result, these managers are reluctant to implement any unknown, untried concept designed to improve the organization's performance. This is where benchmarking steps in, with a proven concept that defines how the organization can close the gap between its performance and the performance of its very best competitors.

Edward Tracy, vice president for AT&T's MMS Division, stated, "Since divestiture, we have been trying to quickly find our way in a very competitive market. Even our internal customers—19 autonomous business units—began asking questions on how our services and cost compared with outside suppliers."

Darel Hall, manager of transportation and planning at AT&T's MMS Division, stated, "AT&T went into benchmarking for the right reason: to improve our business and culture."

Most major organizations around the world invested vast sums of money in the 1980s and 1990s to bring about continuous improvement in their performance. The results were good, and the typical improvement rate has been between 5 and 20 percent a year. Still, many organizations continue to lose their market share and experience decreased profit margins. Now management is beginning to ask themselves,

"How much change is really necessary or possible?" In short, what is the world-class standard for these processes and products?

This is the point at which organizations usually ask, "Is it possible for our processes or products to be better? If so, what can we do to make them better? Don't give us that old stuff about continuous improvement; we want specific implementation advice, not just more theory. Where do we go from here? We have used up all our ideas; maybe we have gone as far as we can go with the improvement process. What we need is a major breakthrough that will decrease costs and error rates by 50 percent now."

Chances are that there still is "gold to mine in them thar hills." To find it, what you need to do now is to look outside your own location at other, similar processes and/or products within your own organization, and at outside organizations as well. Your purpose is to understand what they are doing, and to use this combined experience and knowledge to help improve your process even further. This act of systematically defining the best systems, processes, procedures, and practices is called *benchmarking*. The benchmarking process can improve an item's* performance by as much as 60 percent in less than 12 months (see Fig. 1-1).

Tom Carter, vice president of quality at Alcoa, stated, "We use benchmarking to understand what level of performance is really possible and to understand why the gap exists between our current performance and that optimum performance."

Being the very best in any field is a difficult and lonely road to travel. Once you reach your goal, there is only one

---

*Throughout this book, the word *item* will be used to refer to anything that is being benchmarked, whether it is products, processes, procedures, practices, or equipment.

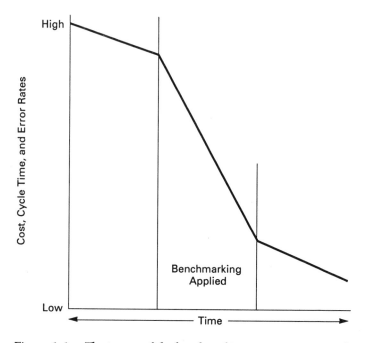

Figure 1-1. *The impact of the benchmarking process on cost, cycle time, and error rates.*

direction to go: *down.* When you are the best, you are envied, undermined, frequently criticized, and expected to outperform the competition no matter what the circumstances. Why then, do so many people, teams, and organizations want to be recognized as the very best? The reasons are simple. Excellence brings:

- Customers
- Employee and management satisfaction
- Recognition
- Higher rewards

- Respect
- Power
- Money

Here are the steps you need to take to become the very best:

1. Know yourself, your strengths, and your limitations.
2. Recognize and understand what the leading organizations do in the area in which you hope to excel.
3. Use the best processes available.
4. Build on these processes to create even better ones.
5. Never stop improving.

The benchmarking process helps you know your organization, understand its competition, define the best processes, and integrate them into your business activities. This book reviews the benchmarking process, and discusses how you can apply it to become a world-class organization that others will want to copy.

The key to any organization's or individual's success is:

- Having meaningful measurements to show how well your organization is performing
- Understanding how well other organizations can perform similar activities (both competitors and noncompetitors)
- Understanding why others perform better than your organization
- Identifying any negative gap between your organization and another organization and taking rapid, effective action to close that gap

Most organizations are faced with the realization that they need to improve such indicators (measurements) as return on assets, market share, customer satisfaction, and net profits. Although these are important measurements that should drive the business, they are resultant measurements and do not reflect the true cause of the problem. Most managers react to negative trends in these major indicators by implementing corrective action to restabilize the organization's pattern, putting it back on track.

Seldom are the organization's targets challenged to be sure they are correct. If the organization was growing at a rate of 5 percent a year and stops, management directs its efforts at reestablishing a 5 percent growth rate, when perhaps the correct figure is a 15 percent growth rate. Budgets are based on last year's budgets, plus a little extra for inflation and/or a little less for improved productivity. Maybe the budget should be 50 percent of what it is right now. Managers try to improve their product introduction cycle and pat themselves on the back if it drops from 18 months to 14 months, when it really should go down to 6 months. The problem is usually threefold:

1. Management does not know how well the different parts of the organization should be performing.

2. Management does not think a major improvement in the organization can be accomplished.

3. Management does not know how to bring about a major improvement in the organization.

The answer to this dilemma is benchmarking. Benchmarking is a powerful tool that provides the organization with measurements of how well products, equipment, people, services, and processes can perform. It allows the organization to realize that it needs to break out of the old mode, and that major improvements not only can be made but must be made if the organization is to survive. Benchmarking also gives the organization a clear understanding of how other organizations are able to perform at superior levels. It provides managers not only with aggressive, realistic goals but also with the confidence that they can achieve these goals because they know that other organizations are doing so. Is it any wonder that benchmarking has become one of the world's most powerful improvement tools?

But is it ethical? Or was *Business Week* right when in 1993 it described benchmarking as "a euphemism for legally ripping off someone else's idea"? Of course benchmarking is legal and ethical, it if is done correctly. The human race has evolved by building upon other people's ideas. We cannot afford the attitude of "It is no good if it not invented here." Creativity is great and provides a great deal of self-satisfaction, but it is also time-consuming and spotty. If someone or some organization has a good idea and is willing to share it with you, take the free gift. Isn't that what education is all about? When we look objectively at benchmarking, it is simply a systematic way of collecting information about equipment, product and/or process performance, then analyzing why some items outperform others and applying this knowledge to improve your organization's performance.

DOES BENCHMARKING WORK FOR ALL ORGANIZATIONS?

Studies at Ernst & Young LLP prove that benchmarking works well for organizations classified as "winners" and "survivors," but not for those classified as "losers" (see Fig. 1-2). Available data suggest that it can be hazardous for organizations classified as losers to use benchmarking. In fact, best-practices process benchmarking can be detrimental to loser organizations, because they need to pay attention to the basics and today's problems rather than focusing on being country class or world class.*

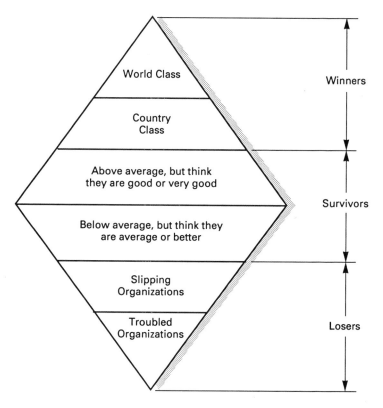

Figure 1-2. *Distribution of organizations according to performance.*

---

*For information on how to determine if your organization is a winner, survivor, or loser, see *Total Improvement Management* (McGraw-Hill, 1995).

In Fig. 1-2, country-class organizations are defined as the top 10 percent in the country in which the benchmarking organization is located. (An example is Ford comparing itself with all U.S. organizations for a specific item.) World-class organizations are the top 10 percent of the organizations in the world. You will note that 50 percent of all organizations are below average. This does not mean that those organizations are not meeting customer requirements. In fact, most of them are, and some of them are even making a profit doing business at the present time.

Figure 1-3 shows the 10 steps to becoming the "best of the best." There can only be *one* "best of the best" (Step 10) for every benchmark item. Most organizations can consider themselves a success if they reach either Step 6 or 7. A few of the very best organizations will reach Step 8 or 9, and that one very special organization will reach Step 10. The benchmarking process is designed to help organizations move up this "stairway to success."

KEY DEFINITIONS AND ABBREVIATIONS

Before we look at the benchmarking process in detail, the following key definitions and abbreviations are in order.

benchmark (BMK): A standard by which an item can be measured or judged.

benchmarking database: The stored collection of essential data assembled by the individual BITs as well as analyzed information. A typical database includes:

• The item's characterization results

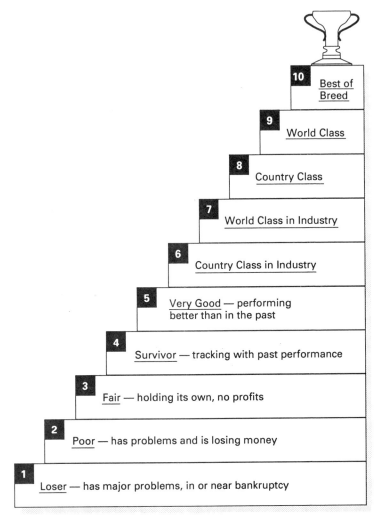

Figure 1-3. *The stairway to success.*

- Survey results
- Summary of data collected from external and internal publications
- The data matrix
- List of improvement opportunities
- Root cause/corrective action analysis
- Gap/trend analysis graphs
- Summary of site visits
- Simulation model
- Flowcharts of the benchmark item
- Measurement interaction charts

benchmarking (BMKG): A systematic way to identify, understand, and creatively evolve superior products, services, designs, equipment, processes, and practices to improve your organization's real performance.

benchmarking implementation team (IT): A group of people assembled during the improvement phase of the benchmarking process in order to implement the improvements developed by the benchmarking item team.

benchmarking initiation team (BT): A small group of people, usually from different functions, who are assigned to get the benchmarking process started, coordinate its implementation, and serve as in-house consultants for the benchmarking activities. Sometimes called the *benchmarking coordination team* (BCT).

benchmark item (BI): The focus of the benchmarking project. The BI may encompass business processes, manufacturing processes, products, services, equipment, and/or computer programs.

benchmarking item team (BIT): The group assigned responsibility to benchmark an individual item. Sometimes called the *benchmarking team.*

benchmarking partner (BP): Any internal or external organization that agrees to cooperate by exchanging data and/or hosting a site visit with the organization that initiated the benchmarking project.

benchmarking plan: A document that is used to define the detailed process that the BIT follows to benchmark a specific item. The benchmarking plan includes:

- Measurement plan
- External and internal data collection plans
- List of external experts
- List of internal and external published information sources that the BIT will or may use
- List of internal and external potential benchmarking partners
- Time-line (Gantt) charts for activities and tasks
- List of internal and external sites that are visited
- Organizational Change Management plan
- List of key contacts
- All detailed work plans
- All potential future-state solutions
- The future-state solution implementation plan

benchmarking process (BMKP): The methodology used to conduct a benchmarking evaluation, analyze the findings, and implement the future-state solution.

best-value future-state solution: The solution that results in the most beneficial redesigned item as viewed by the item's stakeholders. It is the best combination of desired costs and results. Examples include ROI, customer satisfaction, market share, risk, and value-added per employee.

comparative analysis (CPA): The first half of a benchmarking project, during which the organization measures its item's performance and compares it with similar items in other organizations to define the differences in performance. Many organizations confuse comparative analysis with a complete benchmarking process and do not realize this is only the beginning.*

future-state solution (FSS): A combination of corrective actions and changes that can be applied to the item under study to increase its value to its stakeholders.

Organizational Change Management (OCM): The methodology used to manage the implementation of critical or major changes throughout the organization to greatly increase the probability of the changes being implemented effectively and efficiently.

---

*Comparative analysis comprises the first three phases of the five-phase benchmarking process. See Chapter 6 for details.

THE BENCHMARKING OVERVIEW

WHAT IS BENCHMARKING?

Benchmarking is a continuous process of comparison, projection, and implementation. It involves

- Comparing the organization and its parts with the best organizations, regardless of the industry or country
- Comparing business processes with the best similar processes in any or all industries to define best value
- Comparing production processes with the best similar processes in any or all industries to define best value
- Comparing the organization's products and services with those of the best competitors
- Comparing different types of equipment to select the best-value equipment for the specific application
- Implementing defined best practices
- Projecting future trends in best practices and proactively reacting to these trends
- Meeting and exceeding customer/consumer expectations

Here is what benchmarking will do:

1. It will help the organization learn from the experiences of others. No organization has the time or the resources to make all the mistakes itself.

2. It will show the organization how it is performing in comparison to the best.

3. It will identify the organization's weaknesses and strengths.

4. It will help the organization prioritize its improvement activities.

5. It will provide the organization with proven corrective action plans.

Robert C. Camp, in his book *Benchmarking—The Search for Industry Best Practices That Lead to Superior Performance,* has defined the benchmarking process as "the search for industry best practices that lead to superior performance." David T. Kearns, chief executive officer of Xerox Corporation, defines benchmarking as "the continuous process of measuring products, services, and practices against the toughest competition or those companies recognized as industrial leaders." *Webster's Ninth New Collegiate Dictionary* defines benchmarking (benchmark) as "a point of reference from which measurements may be made" and "something that serves as a standard by which others may be measured." For our purposes, benchmarking can be defined as "a systematic way to identify, understand, and evolve superior products, services, designs, equipment, processes, and practices to improve an organization's real performance."

Real performance highlights a unique emphasis that is included in the new benchmarking approach presented here. The concept of striving to be the very best is replaced by the concept of best value to the organization. A benchmarking project that decreases cycle time from 30 days to 3 days, but does not improve market share, value added per employee, return on assets, or customer satisfaction is not a value-added solution. It may bring the organization up to world class in an area that the customer does not care about. In reality, this is wasted effort—effort that should have been applied elsewhere. Benchmarking processes that implement best-value solutions are the ones that bring about real performance improvement.

BENCHMARKING APPROACHES

Benchmarking is a never-ending discovery and learning experience that identifies and evaluates best items in order to integrate their best features into an organization's items. Improvements in effectiveness, efficiency, and adaptability will maximize their value-added contribution to the organization. Competitive benchmarking originally was viewed as simply purchasing competitive products to compare them with the ones manufactured by the purchasing organization. This process (competitive product test and disassembly) is only a small part of the larger benchmarking activity. In this book we will be looking at the whole benchmarking process. We will look at how to benchmark the following:

- Business processes
- Equipment
- Manufacturing (production) processes
- Products and services

Product, manufacturing, process, and equipment benchmarking have been in use since the early 1900s. We have become used to many of these benchmarking tools under the names of competitive analysis, reverse engineering, disassembly analysis, competitive shopping, and so on. The recent focus on benchmarking is driven by the high cost and poor performance of most of America's business processes.

We will examine how to define and understand the best benchmarking practices and processes to enable an organization to provide superior products and/or services at reduced cost. Benchmarking can be applied to almost anything. It is an effective way to improve processes, products, equipment, organizational structure, performance, and systems. In short, anything that is going on in your organization can be benchmarked.

The benchmarking process is a lot like a detective story, and the person doing the benchmarking operates a lot like a detective. He or she must search through the many clues available in the public domain to find leads, then dissect these leads to define root causes. Once the many clues are understood—shazam! They fall together to give the benchmarking team the best-value future-state solution. It can be an exciting and enlightening adventure.

WHY USE BENCHMARKING?

Organizations undertake a benchmarking initiative for a number of reasons. Among them are:

- To set challenging but realistic goals
- To define how goals can be accomplished
- To define gaps between the organization's performance and its competitors' performance

- Because a breakthrough improvement is required to stay competitive
- Because the organization is losing market share and needs to turn around
- To define the pain related to the "as is" item
- Because overhead costs are running too high
- Because the competition's quality is much better
- Because the competition is bringing product to market much faster
- Because one function in the organization is trying to impress upper management
- To test the soundness of the organization's strategy
- Because management feels there is a need to break down the "not invented here" syndrome
- To define competitors' future strategies and resource investment plans
- Because there is a need to supplement the organization's ideas with fresh thoughts
- To overcome management's complacency by exposing inaccurate perceptions
- Because the Malcolm Baldrige Award requires that benchmarking be done
- To find out how the organization measures up against the world's best
- To identify more stringent improvement targets
- To identify organizational strengths and weaknesses
- To help management direct the improvement effort
- To uncover emerging technologies or practices

- To improve stakeholders' satisfaction level
- To learn from the experiences of world-class organizations
- To provide early warning when the organization is falling behind

The two primary reasons for using the benchmarking process are setting goals and identifying how the goals can be accomplished. There is nothing like seeing someone else achieve what was thought to be impossible to make believers out of the most skeptical of us.

Every person, process, and organization needs to set goals that are challenging yet attainable. Without set goals, life becomes confusing and unrewarding. Whether it is in personal matters or business matters, we all want to improve. No one wants to be average. In today's fast-paced, quality-focused business world, being average is just as bad as being poor. Always remember that 50 percent of the people, organizations, and products are below average. Are you sure your organization is not below average?

In the past, goals were usually based on the organization's (or the item's) past performance. This very limited use of internal vision made for little correlation between the organization's goals and the ultimate standard of excellence. Occasionally, the organization's goals exceeded what was achievable, but more commonly they fell far below what had been, or could be, achieved.

Great organizations—from the Roman Empire to IBM— have failed because of incest. They looked inward only, instead of benefiting from the experiences of others. IBM was a national leader in the 1970s. It was number 1 on *Fortune* magazine's list of the most admired corporations for years in the 1980s. By 1993, it had slipped to number 354 out of the 404 corporations listed. That put IBM in the lower 13 percent of the list—a true "riches to rags" story. Higher-ups had been careful not to contaminate themselves with outside influences. Most IBM employees were selected right out of school, so that they were not tainted by other organizations' approaches. The employees felt that IBM had patented its slogan "Think" and that no other organization could do so. As a result, IBM became 50 percent over-staffed, stock dropped from over $150 to about $40 a share in a 3-year period, and dividends tumbled 80 percent, caus-ing major hardships on retired IBM employees. Many retirees had invested 10 percent of their income into IBM stock for decades to ensure security during their golden years. These individuals suddenly found themselves out in the cold. IBM's recent action of replacing the internally grown upper management team with a fresh set of leaders who have a broader view of business is an excellent example of what good organizations need to do to get a fresh start.

Let's compare the record of the old inward-looking IBM with that of the new outward-looking IBM.

	INWARD IBM (CEO AKERS' LAST YEAR—1993)	OUTWARD IBM (CEO GERSTNER'S FIRST YEAR—1994)	% CHANGE
Total revenue	62,716*	64,052	+2.1
Total cost	38,568	38,768	+0.5
Total operating expenses	32,785	20,279	−38.1
Net earnings	(8,101)	3,021	—

*All numbers are in millions of dollars.

During the same 12-month period, the number of regular full-time employees fell from 256,207 to 219,839. Under John

Akers, stock prices dropped to a post–World War II low of around $45 and came back under Louis Gerstner to over $85. This major turnaround was accomplished in a relatively stable market, as the total revenue figures indicate. What IBM had was two very different CEOs faced with the same problem—John Akers, who grew up in the IBM system, and Lou Gerstner, who brought in a fresh perspective.

No organization can survive today without placing major emphasis on understanding the good points of its competition and learning from the best of breed. No organization is the best in all its activities. Every organization in the world has a lot to learn by benchmarking other organizations. Benchmarking injects fresh red blood into anemic blue-blood organizations. The biggest single obstacle that a new benchmarking project faces is convincing management and employees that they can learn something from outside the organization (the not-invented-here syndrome).

By setting low goals for ourselves, we enjoy a false sense of accomplishment. When we do not know how good we should be, improvement within our organization is slow—because we so easily meet the low standards we set for ourselves. As a result, many individuals, processes, and organizations fail to mature to their full potential. Benchmarking is the antidote to this self-imposed mediocrity, because it provides a means for setting challenging goals and attaining these goals.

Even more crucial is the fact that the benchmarking process provides a way to discover and understand methods that can be applied to the organization to bring about major improvements. The unique value of the benchmarking process is that it not only tells you how good you can be, it also tells you how to change the way you are doing business so that you can be that good.

You need to address both functions of the benchmarking process—comparative analysis (the what) and product/system knowledge (the how). What good is defining the gap between your organization and your competitors or world-class organizations if you do not know how to improve your processes to narrow the gap? Knowing that you are inferior, but not being able to improve, just discourages everyone. A proper benchmarking process must be designed to provide both the "what" and the "how."

PROVIDING THE "WHAT"

The importance of measurements cannot be overstressed. Without the ability to measure, you cannot control your organization. Obtaining quantitative data is absolutely essential in the pursuit of becoming, and then staying, world class.

There is no real debate over the importance of measurements. We know that in order to operate effectively, we must be able to measure. The question that needs to be decided, is what should be measured in the benchmarking process. Benchmarking should measure such things as:

- How fast
- How good
- How much
- Where
- When
- How long
- Size, shape, form, and fit

To encourage free exchange of information between organizations, it is often necessary to use ratio measurements whenever applicable. By using ratios instead of real values, you can exchange information with other organizations without having to disclose production rates or absolute values.

In competitive benchmarking, your organization probably will not get the cooperation that is needed from its competitors. In these cases, you need to collect the data yourself using techniques like reverse engineering, competitive shopping, and competitive performance analysis. This information is extremely valuable because it is directly compatible with and comparable to your item's data. Often in competitive benchmarking the organization can make use of third-party test laboratories (such as *Consumer Reports*) to obtain performance comparisons between the item under study and the competitor's item.

Providing the "How"

Another real advantage of the benchmarking process is that it provides insights into how others have become the best. This aspect focuses on discovering how world-class organizations developed their processes and products to ensure superior performance.

At this juncture, you must look at an organization, a product, a process, or an activity, and seek out and analyze the reasons that make it the best of its kind. The specifics you might analyze are:

- The how-to's
- The knowledge
- The ways
- The processes
- The methods

You should then apply this knowledge to your benchmark item, adapting and/or improving it to meet the unique requirements of the customers, employees, and products that make up your organization's personality.

TARGET BEING BETTER THAN THE BEST, OR YOU WILL LOSE

If you simply adopt another organization's approach or adapt it to your item, you will not obtain the desired results. The reason is that as your future-state solution is being implemented, your benchmarking partner's item is also improving. The "copycat" approach to improvement will keep your organization always in a catch-up mode. This means that all future-state solutions must incorporate what the benchmarking partner is doing today and improve upon it before the future-state solution is implemented. The challenge is not as difficult as you might think. No doubt you would implement almost every project you have undertaken a little differently if you had to do it over. This is your chance to further refine the world-class item, while combining the best points from each organization that you benchmark, to set a new standard of excellence.

WHAT BENCHMARKING CAN DO

Benchmarking not only defines how certain items measure up to similar items of competitors and noncompetitors. It also provides the organization with a future-state solution for the negative gaps (see Fig. 2-1). The benchmarking process is not easy. It requires much patience and hard work. And the work never stops. Continuous monitoring is required to keep the database updated. Why, then, should

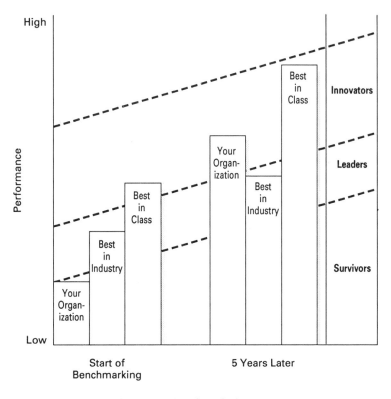

Figure 2-1. *The evolution of a benchmarked item.*

any organization even begin? Because the benefits of benchmarking far outweigh the effort and expense. Here are some of the benefits of benchmarking:

- Increases the desire to change.
- Focuses on meeting end-user expectations.
- Improves the benchmark item.
- Improves key financial indicators.

- Focuses on the use of best worldwide practices.
- Provides a way to improve customer satisfaction.
- Helps eliminate the not-invented-here syndrome.
- Includes the use of proven approaches, methods, processes, and technologies.
- Improves employee morale and pride.
- Improves relationships and understanding between benchmarking partners.
- Identifies your competitive position.
- Identifies strengths and weaknesses.
- Increases the effectiveness, efficiency, and adaptability of your processes.
- Transforms complacency into an urgent desire to improve.
- Defines and incorporates best applicable processes and management practices.
- Helps set attainable, but aggressive, targets.
- Provides breakthrough types of improvement.
- Concentrates on the major contributors to the success of the organization.
- Allows you to project future trends in your industry.
- Sets new standards of performance.
- Prioritizes improvement activities.
- Provides a faster, lower-risk approach to meeting aggressive targets.
- Provides your organization with a competitive advantage.
- Creates a culture of continuous improvement.
- Reduces the cost of the improvement process.
- Develops a professional interface with other organizations.

When organizations start to apply the benchmarking process, a significant internal attitude change takes place.

Before Benchmarking	*After Benchmarking*
Not invented here	Let's use that good idea
One answer to a problem	Many options
Internal focus	External focus
History-based targets	Best-performance targets
Low market understanding	High market understanding
Internal priorities	Customer priorities
Reactive improvements	Proactive improvements
Problem focus	Opportunity focus
Driven by personality	Driven by best industry practices
Path of least resistance	Best-value path
We are good	We need to be better
Managed by experience	Managed by facts
Following the industry	Leading the industry

HISTORY OF THE BENCHMARKING PROCESS

No one truly knows the origin of benchmarking (the comparison of one item to another to set a standard for excellence). It is easy to imagine Adam comparing the apple Eve gave him with the other apples on the tree to be sure it was the biggest and the reddest. It is easy to see that the concept of benchmarking was known in China as early as the fourth century B.C. by reading the works of Sun Tzu, author of *The Art of War*. Sun Tzu wrote, "If you know the enemy and you know yourself, your victory will not stand in doubt." Indeed, throughout the ages the human race has evaluated the strengths and weaknesses of others to make a decision on how to avoid situations which would not have a positive outcome.

Benchmark is a surveyor's term that has been around for hundreds of years. Surveyors used benchmarks as key reference points of previously determined positions that other boundaries were referred back to. From a product standpoint, benchmarking has been used since the early 1900s to understand how the competition was building its products and how well the competitor's product functioned. The Japanese brought the benchmarking concept to new heights after World War II when they toured the world, benchmarking all the best organizations. For the first time, the focus was not on product, but on process. The Japanese didn't call it benchmarking; they called it "industry tours." But the process was the same:

1. Research published data to define the best.
2. Contact the best and schedule a visit.
3. Visit the best and carefully select pertinent data.
4. Return home and adopt the lessons learned in the Japanese organization (or adapt them) to gain a competitive advantage.

Today in Japan, benchmarking has fallen out of favor. Why? Because the Japanese use benchmarking to identify best practices and *adapt* them to their item. Most Japanese organizations feel that *copying* another organization's products, processes, or procedures ensures falling behind that organization because of the time required to implement the future-state solution.

IBM

IBM began its internal benchmarking activities in the early 1960s, because it saw a great deal of variation in performance among locations. To get the process started, IBM established key indicator measurements for each function (development engineering, product engineering, personnel, quality assurance, accounting, customer engineering, and so on). Once a year, key measurements were reported to corporate headquarters. Typical measurements included:

- New product release cycle time
- Ratio of quality inspectors to manufacturing operators
- Span of control
- Maintenance cost as a percentage of equipment cost
- R&D cost per patent

Between 8 and 16 measurements were developed per function, and these measurements were turned in to corporate headquarters, which would analyze and plot the data to compare all locations. The reports were then returned to all locations, and the locations that had a negative gap were asked to study the better-performing locations and explain to corporate headquarters what could be done to reduce this gap.

Individuals who had to answer these reports faced many challenges. Unfortunately, the people who answered a particular report often spent more time defining why they were different and could not change than looking at how they could really improve. Although the program did some good, the benefits that it should have generated were not realized because of lack of follow-through on management's part at the local and corporate levels.

During the late 1960s, IBM came to the conclusion that its overall production cost structure could be significantly reduced if it could adopt the best existing practices at its worldwide locations. Beyond just the cost issue, IBM saw that the quality and consistency of its products would improve dramatically. To accomplish this plan, a corporate directive was written requiring all process-sensitive products to be manufactured by compatible processes. The result was a corporatewide effort to have common practices at all IBM plants. If this plan proved impractical, then at the very least processes had to be compatible among locations, thereby ensuring interchangeability of product at any point within the process. IBM gained a significant international competitive advantage through its ability to determine the best production processes internally and adopt them as the corporate standard.

XEROX

In the late 1970s, Xerox decided to follow IBM's example by comparing its U.S. products with those of its Japanese affiliate, Fuji-Xerox. Management was humbled to learn that Fuji-Xerox was selling copiers at a price equivalent to what it cost U.S. Xerox simply to manufacture the copiers. This lesson was the spark that started a successful program aimed at reducing costs in Xerox's U.S. manufacturing process. The initial benchmarking program was so successful that management later incorporated it as a fundamental element in Xerox's worldwide improvement efforts.

This improvement process was so pronounced that Xerox is often credited as being the forerunner of the benchmarking movement. In Xerox's program, benchmarking took on new dimensions. As techniques were applied to areas beyond product processes, such as support processes, Xerox discovered that benchmarking could be used in any area of the organization. The company went beyond benchmarking itself or even its competition, and opened the sphere of potential benchmarking partners to any organization that performed a similar activity. Benchmarking was a major contributor to stopping Xerox's declining market share (losing over 30 percent of its market during the 1970s and early 1980s) and initiating a comeback (regaining over 10 percent of the market in the past 10 years).

MOTOROLA AND BEYOND

Today, many organizations have built upon the works of such early pioneers as IBM and Xerox, and have used benchmarking to help drive their continuous improvement efforts. One shining example is Motorola, which cites benchmarking as one of the major tools powering its improvement process. In 1988, Motorola received the prestigious Malcolm Baldrige Award for its quality improvement efforts. Feel assured that benchmarking played no small role in the Malcolm Baldrige Award examining committee's decision.

The following is a partial list of other organizations that are deeply involved in the benchmarking process:

Alcoa	Hewlett-Packard
Allied Signal	Hughes Aircraft
AT&T	John Deere
Bell Atlantic	Johnson & Johnson
Boeing	L. L. Bean
Caterpillar	Milliken
Digital Equipment Corporation	NCR
Du Pont	Procter & Gamble
Eastman Kodak	3M
Florida Power & Light	Wallace

THE PROCESS OF BENCHMARKING

TYPES OF BENCHMARKING

There are five types of benchmarking processes. They are:

- Internal benchmarking
- External competitive benchmarking
- External industry (compatible) benchmarking
- External generic (transindustry) benchmarking
- Combined internal and external benchmarking

Table 3-1 shows the benchmarking partners' relative cooperation, the applicability of the data collected, and the degree of breakthrough the organization will get using the different types of benchmarking.

There is no "best" benchmarking type. Each of the different types (internal, external competitive, external industry, external generic, and combined internal and external) has its own advantages and disadvantages that need to be considered.

INTERNAL BENCHMARKING

Internal benchmarking is the starting point and should always be considered before any organization looks to the

TABLE 3-1   A Comparison of Types of Benchmarking

TYPE OF BENCHMARKING	COOPERATION	RELEVANCE OF INFORMATION	DEGREE OF BREAKTHROUGH
Internal	High	High	Low
External competitive	Low	High	Medium
External industry	Medium	Medium	High
External generic	Medium	Low	High
Combined internal and external	Medium	Medium	Very high

outside. If an organization is just starting its benchmarking program, internal benchmarking is an excellent way to develop the benchmarking process and train people in how to use it. This approach is very effective in organizations that have many small business units and/or relatively autonomous sites that are engaged in similar activities.

Internal benchmarking involves looking within the organization to determine if other locations are performing similar activities, and then defining the best practices observed. This type of benchmarking is the easiest to conduct because there are no security and/or confidentiality problems to overcome. In almost all cases, internal benchmarking should be undertaken first, since it is inexpensive to conduct and provides detailed data. Even better, the organization can frequently borrow experienced personnel from other locations to help implement the future-state solutions.

As early as 1978, IBM had a corporate policy that required all process-sensitive products to be benchmarked worldwide at least once a year. This approach involved detailed studies down to the task level to ensure that all differences were identified and understood. At IBM in San Jose,

California, the effort was led by a quality engineering team made up of manufacturing engineers, test engineers, and product engineers.

EXTERNAL COMPETITIVE BENCHMARKING

External competitive benchmarking is an effective approach in industries that are very competitive, industries whose competitors have very different management philosophies and histories, and industries that are driven by emerging technologies and processes. The reverse engineering and competitive shopping approaches that are part of this type of benchmarking are very important to organizations whose output is hard or soft goods. Organizations using external competitive methods need to be experienced in benchmarking.

Competitive benchmarking, which includes reverse engineering and competitive shopping, requires that the organization perform a detailed analysis of a competitor's products, services, and processes. The most common approach is to purchase competitive products and services, then analyze them to identify competitive advantages.

Originally, some organizations were apprehensive about the ethics involved in this process. Today, however, few organizations can compete without a thorough understanding of the competition's products and services. Even such organizations as IBM, Xerox, General Motors, and Hewlett-Packard make effective use of this method. In fact, most auto manufacturers carefully disassemble competitive cars and place them piece by piece in rows to compare their designs and assembly methods.

Competitive products are extensively tested to identify their strengths and weaknesses, and to generate performance profiles. A thorough competitive benchmarking process also reviews key information not directly related to the product. Close examination of the packaging, operating manuals, service instructions, and delivery methods can provide a great deal of valuable information.

EXTERNAL INDUSTRY (COMPATIBLE) BENCHMARKING

External industry benchmarking compares the benchmark item with items produced by the world's best organizations in a general industry category (examples: banking, insurance, health care, electronics). In this case, the benchmarking partner's item does not compete directly for the same customers. This type of benchmarking is used when organizations feel they have something to gain by comparing their benchmark item with compatible items in other organizations that are engaged in the same industry but are not direct competitors. Organizations using industrial benchmarking should already be familiar with the benchmarking process.

EXTERNAL GENERIC (TRANSINDUSTRY) BENCHMARKING

External generic (transindustry) benchmarking extends the benchmarking process outside the specific organization and its industry, to involve dissimilar industries. Many business processes are generic in application and extend across industries (examples: warehousing, supplier relations, service parts logistics, advertising, customer relations, hiring). Applying the benchmarking process to these generic items can provide meaningful insights, particularly when the information comes from unrelated industries. Benchmarking dissimilar industries enables you to discover innovative processes, not currently used in your particular product types, that will allow your process to become the best of breed.

COMBINED INTERNAL AND EXTERNAL BENCHMARKING

The most frequently used approach is the combination of internal and external (competitive, industry, and/or generic) benchmarking. This combination usually produces the best results. Table 3-2 shows a comparison of the different benchmarking types.

SETTING BENCHMARKING PARTNER LIMITS

Setting some limitations on the organizations to be benchmarked will provide meaningful results at lower cost, however. Some restrictions you may want to consider are:

- *Customer requirements*—high quality and reliability; or low-quality, one-time usage

TABLE 3-2   A Comparison of Different Benchmarking Types

BENCHMARKING TYPE	CYCLE TIME FOR FSS*	BENCHMARKING PARTNERS	RESULTS
Internal	3–4 months	Within the organization	Major improvements
External competitive	6–12 months	None	Better than the competition
External industry	10–14 months	Same industry	Creative breakthrough
External generic	12–24 months	All industries worldwide	Changes the rules
Combined internal and external	12–24 months	All industries worldwide	Best in class

*FSS = future-state solution.

TABLE 3-3   Typical Benchmark Organizations Identified by Xerox

ORGANIZATION	PRODUCT/PROCESS BENCHMARK CATEGORY
Canon	Copiers
DEC	Work stations
L. L. Bean	Warehouse operations
General Electric	Information systems
Deere	Service parts logistics
Ford	Assembly automation generic processes
Federal Reserve	Bill scanning
Citicorp	Document processing

SOURCE: Robert C. Camp, *Benchmarking—The Search for Industry Best Practices That Lead to Superior Performance* (ASQC Quality Press, 1989), p. 62.

- *Product characteristics*—size, shape, weight, environment, and so on.

- *Output usage*—broad industrial categories, not specific products: grocery industry, office products industry, electronics industry, transportation industry, and so on.

The benchmarking process can be applied to a product, a process, a subprocess, or even an individual activity. Xerox has actively applied the benchmarking process at all levels. Table 3-3 lists some of the benchmark organizations it has identified.

THE BENCHMARKING PROCESS

Very simply, the benchmarking process involves

- Deciding what will be benchmarked

- Defining the items to compare
- Developing measurements to compare
- Defining internal sites, and external organizations, to benchmark
- Collecting and analyzing data
- Determining the gap between your item and the best item
- Developing action plans, targets, and measurement processes
- Updating the benchmarking effort

WHAT SHOULD BE BENCHMARKED?

There are two different benchmarking approaches: strategic benchmarking and organizational benchmarking. Most organizations need to use both of them.

STRATEGIC BENCHMARKING.   Under the strategic approach, major portions of the organization are benchmarked to identify weaknesses and strengths within a specific area or functional unit. For example, the financial function could benchmark its activities to define internal weaknesses. The strategic benchmarking process is usually followed by a series of very specific benchmarking activities, such as benchmarking the billing process.

ORGANIZATIONAL BENCHMARKING.   When the organizational approach is used, considerable research has already been expended to be sure that the benchmarking projects will support the business plan and are directed at items that, if improved, will impact the organization's competitive position. Examples include soldering process benchmarking, order-entry process benchmarking, and drive-motor assembly benchmarking.

As a starting point, benchmark all your customer interfaces. Don't limit your benchmarking to products. Your reputation is based on every contact your customer has with anything relating to your organization. This includes the contract trucker who delivers your product to a customer's warehouse, the way you answer your telephones, the accuracy of your bills, the responsiveness of your sales force, and the effectiveness of your service team. In addition, you should benchmark all your critical business processes, as well as key subprocesses and activities. Consider benchmarking your product, manufacturing process, equipment, and business processes.

Another key place to obtain direction on what to benchmark is the organization's business plan. The benchmarking process should support the business plan and its critical success factors. Once the appropriate information has been collected and the projects have been defined, the benchmarking process should become part of the business plan. Often, benchmarking provides the key input to the organization's objectives, goals, and critical success factors.

From a small group's standpoint, the process differs slightly. After reviewing the business plan and defining its own impact upon that plan, the small group will use a tool called *area activity analysis* to define its customers and critical measurements. When the area activity analysis is completed, the group will select benchmarking projects that are within its span of control, that are relatively significant, and that support the business plan.

PROCESS DESIGN/PLANNING

Tom Carter, vice president of Alcoa, states, "Many people think that benchmarking is simply going out and studying other companies, but you must do a lot of homework before you go out."

A well-designed plan will save you a lot of time and headaches, and provide you with much better results. When an organization starts talking about benchmarking, the impulse is to run out and visit other organizations that could have a better way of doing things. Although this approach is something to be considered, it is not the starting point. Select the items you want to benchmark very carefully. Be sure the items you select are important ones that, if improved, will give your organization a competitive advantage. Then take time to characterize each item before you contact people outside your organization.

The first step is to thoroughly understand your organization. You are in a much better position to start the benchmarking process if you have been involved in business process improvement activities. You have flow-diagrammed your processes, established effectiveness and efficiency measurements, and defined the interrelationships and the dependencies of your processes. All this will help you develop your benchmarking approach.

As you develop your benchmarking plan, do not forget to include the concept of *Organizational Change Management** in the plan. Organizational Change Management needs to start as soon as the item is selected to be benchmarked. Having an effective process of Organizational Change Management, one that prepares the individual who will be impacted by the change, is an essential part of successful benchmarking. Each phase of the benchmarking plan, be it big or small, should include a formal written plan for Organizational Change Management.†

---

*Trademark of Ernst & Young LLP.

†For additional information on Organizational Change Management, see *The Complete Benchmarking Implementation Guide* (McGraw-Hill, 1996).

The plan for Organizational Change Management, at a very minimum, should include the following:

- Definition and communication of the cost of the status quo
- A clearly communicated understanding of the future-state solution
- A map of Organizational Change Management that defines people's roles as:

  Initiating sponsors
  Sustaining sponsors
  Change agents
  Change targets
  Advocates

- Organizational Change Management training to support each individual's role
- Training on how emotions are impacted by a particular change and how to control them
- Change of culture alignment
- Considerations of potential internal and external events that can have a negative impact on the desired change
- A transitional change management plan

KEY COMPARISONS

The next phase of the benchmarking process is to closely evaluate the elements comprising the items being benchmarked. Identify items that

- Have weaknesses within them
- Have a high potential for improvement

- Are sources of delay
- Take a large portion of the total effort
- Are the source of problems

Highlight these focus activities in the benchmarking study.

MEASUREMENTS

Keep the list of key measurements you wish to benchmark as simple as possible. Do not use special terms uncommon to your industry. Analyze the types of data sources commonly available in your industry and/or those measurements considered best professional practices. Base your measurement requirements on this information and/or on accepted industrial standards. You have the most control over your own data, and it is often easier to reformat than to get your benchmarking partners to provide data in your format. At this point, do not worry about the confidentiality of the measurements. At a later date, however, this subject will become very important. Remember that ratio-type measurements are often best for the benchmarking process. Effectiveness and efficiency measurements are key.

BENCHMARKING TARGET LOCATIONS AND/OR ORGANIZATIONS

The benchmarking process generally starts by analyzing the best of the organization's internal operations. Many organizations have parallel operations performed at the same locations or at different locations throughout the world. The process should begin by assembling and sharing information about parallel activities. These parallel operations may decide to form a team to develop, implement, and share the knowledge and cost of the benchmarking process. Often, a great deal of information can be obtained by studying internal operations that, while not exactly the same, use similar methods, for example,

- Customer service problem reporting and in-process quality assurance reporting
- Order processing and purchase requests processing

In addition, internal experts on the benchmark item—people who are close to the technology and probably are involved in outside professional society activities—usually can provide the names of potential benchmarking partners and key contacts within these organizations. The list can be refined during the data collection and analysis stage.

DATA
COLLECTION
AND ANALYSIS

DATA COLLECTION

Two main ways to obtain data are retrieving published data
(completed research) that is in the public domain (books,
magazine articles, technical reports), and conducting original research (interviews, testing/disassembling competitive
products, site visits, surveys). You probably will need to use
both methods in developing your database. Evaluate each
data source carefully for the following:

- Reliability and accuracy
- Availability
- Cost
- Coverage
- Timeliness
- Usefulness
- Usability
- Source
- Level of backup

Your data collection system should first focus on collecting
internal data to thoroughly understand how the items within

your organization are working before you approach external benchmark organizations. One location within a big corporation asked one of its customers to become its benchmarking partner, only to find out that the customer had selected one of the corporation's other locations as the best practice for the same process. Information may be acquired from many sources:

- Internal experts
- Public domain literature
- Professional and trade associations
- Consultants
- Universities
- Other external experts
- Surveys
- Focus groups
- Location visits
- Competitive product evaluation
- Reverse engineering (disassembly analysis)
- Competitive service analysis

This is the order in which information is normally searched out. Do not rule out the use of third-party personnel to do the research work for you. They have the advantage of being able to keep individual responses anonymous.

Internal Experts

One very useful source of information about the item under study is subject-matter experts within your organization. Their review of the benchmarking plan often highlights key points that were overlooked by the BIT. These internal experts are also an excellent source of potential benchmarking partners and frequently can introduce the BIT to key people within the potential benchmarking partner's organization.

RESEARCH LITERATURE

A good librarian can make the research process flow smoothly. Huge databases can be sorted by key words to identify articles, publications, reports, and books on the subject under study. Most of these databases list the documents and include a short summary. The organizations maintaining these business and technical databases can provide you with copies of the desired articles at very reasonable prices.

The best literature sources used in the benchmarking process include:

- Annual reports
- 10K data
- Public magazines
- Industrial journals
- Newspapers
- Periodicals
- Special reports
- Trade publications
- General magazines (*Newsweek, Time,* and so on)
- Association reports and studies
- Association publications
- Books
- Conference proceedings

These data will enhance your understanding of processes used outside your organization, and provide you with key contacts in the best organizations. At a minimum, your research should cover the last 10 years.

RESEARCH PROFESSIONAL AND TRADE ASSOCIATIONS

Do not overlook professional associations as an important source of information. The number of professional and trade associations is surprisingly high. Your local library has an encyclopedic listing. You can be almost certain that some professional or trade association has been formed to understand the process you are benchmarking and has experts in the field. A telephone conversation or a visit to an association's headquarters is time well spent, because the organization may have valuable data or be engaged in important activities related to the benchmark item, which include:

- Conferences
- Association libraries
- Databases
- Field trips
- Reports and publications

RESEARCH CONSULTANTS

Consultants continuously search for the best systems, procedures, and practices, and the nature of their work provides them with the opportunity to observe firsthand the operations of many different organizations in different environments.

A consultant who is actively involved in making an organization's process work (not just teaching) can provide you with an unbiased view of the total process, and the individual steps within the process. Frequently, when you discuss a process with a benchmark organization's employees, they will point out all the good things and let all the bad things go unmentioned. They show you how the process *should* be operating, not how it *is* operating. A consultant, on the other hand, can provide you with a view of the process that is not colored by an employee's natural pride in his or her organization.

Another advantage is that consultants can act as third parties, providing data without divulging specific sources. Frequently organizations hesitate to release information that can be compared with that of other organizations because they are afraid of looking less effective, efficient, or capable. A consultant provides the veil of anonymity necessary to obtain the full cooperation of the targeted benchmark organization. The consultant can ensure that the organization's name will not be associated with unfavorable comparisons.

In practice, holding back the names of organizations that are not world class does not present a problem, because you are trying to identify the best organizations, not compare yourself with another organization. The best organization is usually willing to be listed as such and will give the consultant permission to use its name and document its process. A typical report from your consultant might read, "Ten organizations were benchmarked. Culinar had the best fixture changeover methods and procedures. . . ."

RESEARCH UNIVERSITIES AND OTHER EXPERT SOURCES

Other valuable sources of data include:

- Universities (and their professors)
- Company watchers (brokerage firms)
- Software firms
- Research organizations

Universities and their professors can be important data sources. Former professors provide an especially rich source of research information. These professors often maintain close contacts with students who have graduated and moved into key positions in business and government. In addition, summer study programs and university research projects present a mine of information.

Among the most prized sources of information are the brokerage firms that assign employees the sole task of collecting and analyzing data related to an industry and/or organization. These people can offer insights into an organization and target key contacts.

Software firms get deeply involved in many processes as they apply their products to different organizations. For example, they must thoroughly understand the organization's processes when they are applying software to the order entry, design release, and materials management processes. This close working relationship with these key processes in many organizations puts the software firm in a good position to identify which organizations have the best processes.

There are many organizations that are either governmentally or privately funded to study specific subjects in order to define best practices and evolve new breakthrough approaches. These research organizations often have an excellent grasp of today's state of the art and which organizations are "pushing the envelope."

MAKE FINAL SELECTION OF BENCHMARKING ORGANIZATIONS

Now is the time to review all the data collected and to update your quantitative and qualitative matrixes. Identify any voids existing in the collected data. After a detailed analysis of the data, pinpoint key organizations for benchmarking and identify major contacts there.

By now you should have reduced your potential bench-marking partners to three to five organizations. An organization that looked good at first may be dropped from the list because of

- Unwillingness to share data
- Lack of data
- Existence of better candidates
- Reputation as not being the best performer
- Process not comparable to yours
- Communication problems
- Travel costs
- Lack of interest in the organization

CONDUCT SURVEYS

You are still not ready to make your first visit to a benchmarking organization. There remains one more approach to be considered—one that uncovers far better data at much lower cost. This is the *benchmarking survey.* Surveys administered through a third party will ensure anonymity. They also are an effective and economical way of obtaining qualitative and quantitative data. Third-party surveys offer several advantages:

1. All parties can remain anonymous.
2. The questionnaire is designed to provide all the desired information.
3. The person being surveyed has time to collect the required data, making the responses significantly more accurate.
4. The questionnaire can be designed to avoid ambiguous answers.

5. More extensive information can be collected than is available during a location visit.

6. Written data are usually more accurate than verbal remarks.

Hard, cold facts are always much more valuable than a best guess, and a best guess is often what you get when you ask a question that a person is not prepared to answer. Developing a well-prepared questionnaire is a science, not a matter of luck. Have your professional people draft the questions to be asked, and engage a research professional to design the actual questionnaire.

Model the questionnaire to ensure that you obtain the data that you need. The way questions are worded can greatly impact the way they are answered. For example, consider how the same person responded to the following questions:

QUESTION 1.   How satisfied are you with the software you are using?

ANSWER.   Very satisfied.

QUESTION 2.   Rate the software you are using, compared with the very best, on a scale of 1 to 10, with 1 as bad and 10 as exceptional.

ANSWER.   About average, or 5.

Five types of questions can be used in a questionnaire:

- Multiple choice
- Scale ("On a scale of 1 to 10, with 1 as low and 10 as exceptional, how would you rate your organization's feedback form?")
- Written comments

- Rating
- Forced choice (true/false; yes/no)

Do not ask for proprietary information or for data that your organization would not willingly share with benchmarking partners.

Surveys can be conducted by mail, telephone, face-to-face interview, or any combination of the above. For the best results, follow these steps:

1. Get in touch with the identified contact at each organization in advance to explain why the survey is being conducted and how the data will be used. The organization should be invited to participate as a benchmarking partner. Remember that it takes time and money to fill out the questionnaire, so there should be something in it for the benchmarking organization and for the individuals doing the work. Frequently, providing a copy of the final report serves as the necessary incentive.

2. Mail the survey to the individual. Enclose a self-addressed, stamped return envelope.

3. When the survey is returned, review it in detail and contact the key person to acknowledge its receipt and to clarify any unclear points.

4. Add the data collected from the survey to your database. At the end of the survey phase, all the nonproprietary blanks in your qualitative and quantitative matrixes should be filled in.

5. Send your contact a copy of the final report, a specially prepared comparison of the specific organization with other benchmarking organizations, and a thank-you letter.

Hold Focus Group Meetings

Another effective way to collect and evaluate data is to invite interested parties from different organizations or environments to meet and discuss the process under investigation. Such a *focus group* directs its discussions solely to the process in question. It is best to have a third party organize and facilitate this exchange of information.

Focus groups not only set up standards for the present, but also discuss and evaluate future process changes. Even after the initial study is concluded, it is a good idea to hold periodic focus group meetings. These meetings generate a continuous flow of new ideas and allow the parties involved to benefit from the experiments conducted at the individual locations.

To make the focus group successful, use a third-party facilitator who is well schooled in group dynamics. Carefully select the participants to ensure that they are at the same technical level, and hold the group meetings at a neutral site. Distribute agendas well in advance of the meetings and document the proceedings.

Conduct Location Visits

Seeing is believing, and a location visit can be one of the most exciting parts of the benchmarking process. It is your chance to sit down face to face with your counterparts in other organizations to discuss the processes with which you are all involved. This tour of a benchmarking partner's facility provides your team with an opportunity to observe methods, processes, procedures, equipment, and results firsthand. Because it may be your one chance to get an inside view of what your process could evolve to, you must make the most of every moment you spend at the benchmarking partner's location. A lot of planning should take place before you arrive at the organization's reception desk.

The location visit can be divided into six phases:

- Planning
- Arranging the visit
- Visiting the benchmarking partner
- Debriefing
- Following up
- Preparing and distributing a final report to the benchmarking partner

PLANNING.   By now your database should contain a complete file of the benchmarking organization and the process being studied. Each of the people who will be visiting the organization should prepare and study a complete data file on the benchmarking partner. Then prepare a questionnaire and a visit agenda. Assign each member of the visitation team a specific process activity to investigate. This does not mean that all members will not be alert to the total process, only that the assigned individual will prepare himself or herself to study a given activity and during the visit actively collect data, procedures, and methods related to that area. This approach provides the best process coverage in the shortest period of time.

ARRANGING THE VISIT.   Arrangements are an important part of the visitation cycle. Do not make the initial contact without careful preparation. The first problem is finding the right contact.

Sometimes a business relationship already exists. Perhaps the benchmarking partner is your customer or a supplier. Your organization's representative (sales manager, account manager, or purchasing agent) often can provide a friendly contact that will lead to the key individual responsible for the process you are studying.

Another effective approach is to have a professional make contact with his or her counterpart in the benchmarking partner's firm. Frequently, articles prepared by the benchmarking partner on the subject will open the door. Another way to locate a contact is through professional associations.

After you identify the contact, it is best to make a phone call to introduce yourself. Explain the purpose of the project and describe how the data will be used. Point out that the contact, and the potential benchmarking organization, will benefit from investing time and effort in a location visit. Ask for permission to visit, review the organization's process, and discuss how it functions. Ask if the contact is willing to fill out a questionnaire to provide advance information so that the visit can run more efficiently. (Having the questionnaire returned to you in advance will minimize the time required for the visit. A questionnaire may not be necessary, however, if the potential benchmarking partner participated in the benchmarking survey.)

If the potential benchmarking partner agrees, send a letter documenting the discussion and requesting a date for the visit. The letter should include the questionnaire, information about your process, the names and titles of the people who will be making the visit, and a proposed agenda. Never ask the benchmarking organization to disclose information that your organization would be reluctant to disclose. If you want to meet with particular people or functional units, communicate this request in the letter. Frequently, it is advantageous to take pictures of the process under study and to audiotape the discussions. If you desire to do so, be sure to get prior permission.

VISITING THE BENCHMARKING PARTNER. For best results, limit the visitation team to two to eight people and identify the role of each individual in advance. Also, make sure your list of questions includes only need-to-know information. Show up a little early. It is better to wait than be late. Make the meeting an information-sharing experience. Review the process flow and the data in a conference room, then tour the location to see firsthand what is going on. Talk to employees. Learn how people feel. Look for activities that set this organization apart. Concentrate on understanding these activities. You may want to divide the visitation team into small groups to focus on specific details and individual activities. For example, your data-processing expert might want to meet with the benchmarking organization's programmers.

Use the time after the tour to share your observations and review the data collected. Discuss your benchmarking partner's plans to improve its present process. This is a key conversation and should help to project future process changes. Before you leave the benchmarking organization, extend an invitation to its team to visit your location and observe your process firsthand.

DEBRIEFING. Hold a meeting the same day as the visit to consolidate thinking and document observations. Do not put off the meeting even one day. It may be necessary to stay overnight and fly back the next day, but the time is well spent. Do not take a chance that any single observation will be forgotten. You are looking for process refinements and often a seemingly small element may provide the key that unlocks your future success. After the team returns home, each member should prepare an individual report and add pertinent data to the database.

Following Up. Within a week of your visit, send a letter thanking your contact and extending an invitation for his or her team to visit your location. Point out the very best practices you observed during the visit. Consider inviting the benchmarking organization to join a network that shares best practices on the process being studied on an ongoing basis. Provide the benchmarking partner with a target date by which the final benchmarking report will be received.

Preparing and Distributing a Final Report to the Benchmarking Partner. Prepare and distribute a report comparing the benchmarking partner to the total population. For example, the report could read:

> Of the 10 organizations studied, your order-entry process was rated number 3. The number 1 organization has the following features. . . . TFW Corporation was rated first in this area. Mr. James Harris has agreed to provide the benchmarking partner with details of TFW's process. His telephone number is 212-555-3333. The following matrix shows key process measurements. You will note that the high, low, average, and your organization's data are reported for each measurement.

Evaluate Competitive Products

Competitive product evaluation is designed to answer the question "How good are our competitors' products compared with our products?" Or "Where do our competitors' products outperform our products and where do they have a market advantage?" These are important questions that must be answered for any organization to survive today. Unfortunately, most of your competitors will not share the required information with you. Even if they would, you probably would not want to reciprocate. When you are faced with such "hostile" benchmarking partners, your organization will need to develop the required comparative information itself. Typical information that needs to be collected to compare products includes:

- Operating performance levels
- Reliability performance
- Repair strategy
- Key failure modes
- Ease of use
- Adaptability to environmental changes
- Precision
- Production cost

To collect this type of information, organizations purchase competitive products to test and analyze. These products are subjected to a series of environmental and life tests to measure competitive performance. When failures occur, detailed analyses are conducted to uncover the weaknesses. Typical tests include:

- Temperature and humidity cycling
- Vibration testing
- Acoustical noise analysis
- High-potential testing
- Life testing
- Accelerated life testing
- Environmental stress analysis
- Overload protection analysis
- Safety protection analysis

A control sample of your product is tested in parallel with the competitor's product so that the items' performance can be compared. These tests isolate weaknesses in your organization's design and manufacturing processes. Corrective action can then be taken to eliminate the competitor's advantage.

USE REVERSE ENGINEERING

The logical follow-up to competitive product evaluation is reverse engineering. These studies evaluate competitive samples by carefully disassembling the benchmarking partner's product and comparing it with the organization's item at each level of disassembly. Typical points evaluated are:

- Suppliers used
- Number of parts used
- Assembly/manufacturing approaches
- Ease of repair
- Materials used

Reverse engineering studies often define many improvement opportunities that are instrumental in closing competitive gaps. It is a benchmarking tool that most organizations use today. For example, Motorola applied reverse engineering in developing its mobile phone and Bandit pagers. Xerox has a competitive evaluation laboratory in one corner of its Webster, N.Y., plant where, at almost any time, you can see 20 to 30 competitive products being carefully disassembled, with each of their parts characterized. At IBM's San Jose location, the development laboratory provides this service to the rest of the engineering facility.

ENGAGE IN COMPETITIVE SERVICE ANALYSIS (COMPETITIVE SHOPPING)

It is just as important to understand the difference between competitive service levels and your service level as it is to understand the difference in product performance. Here again, your competitors will probably be reluctant, if not hostile, benchmarking partners. The answer in the service industry is again to buy the competitor's service. This is called *competitive shopping* and is used throughout the world. Safeway markets have a list of products that they can price out against other supermarkets to determine cost differentials. Department managers at the Emporium price out name brands at Macy's to be sure that they are not being undersold and that they are getting the best price from their suppliers. Hotels, banks, and airlines buy competitive services and have their people stay in competitors' hotels, open accounts at competitors' banks, and ride on competitors' airlines. These competitive shoppers measure the competitor's performance against their own organization's performance. In Japan, too, bank employees regularly use competitive bank services to compare their bank's performance against the competitive bank's standards. Typical points to be evaluated include:

- Wait time
- Ease of use
- Cleanliness
- Customer interface process
- Noise level
- Cost
- Accuracy

- Employee capability and knowledge
- Reliability
- Predictability

In the service sector, competitive shopping is required to define the level of performance needed to compete in today's fierce market and to determine where improvement opportunities exist. It is a type of benchmarking that every service organization must repeat almost monthly.

Although many organizations develop their own staff of competitive benchmarkers, there are organizations that specialize in this activity. Evaluation Systems for Personnel (ESP) is one of these organizations. ESP provides internal and external competitive shopping data to their customers throughout the United States. Its competitive benchmarkers are known as *mystery shoppers*. Gerry Blumenthal, president of ESP, defines the organization's activities as follows:

> A mystery shopper is an individual who enters a place of business, posing as a regular customer, whose sole aim it is to evaluate the level of service or sales ability.
>
> We at ESP have developed mystery-shopping questionnaires for almost every industry. Each question in our questionnaires is scored and weighted according to its specific importance. This enables us to evaluate, quantitatively, the service rendered by that specific industry or its salesperson. Thus we are able to measure performances between departments or individuals comprising a company or between different companies. This provides a tool for companies to determine where they stand in relation to the competition. The competition, if they excel in the industry, can then be mystery-shopped to "collect or learn their secrets." In effect, then, the competition has become a *benchmark*.

During the past 8 years we have, through the eyes and ears of over 8000 mystery shoppers, established the specific "things" that people in service or sales do or do not do, in their interaction with customers or clients. Naturally, we come into contact with all levels of operators, including the most successful operators.

By examining these successful operators we have established the *benchmarks* for each industry. Many companies are now actively shopping the competition, specifically for this reason.

DATA ANALYSIS

Data analysis is a critical phase of the benchmarking process, because you must organize masses of numbers and statements into coherent, usable information to direct all your future activities. The success or failure of the benchmarking process depends on how well the reams of collected data are translated into usable information.

The measurement data provide you with indicators of where the best practices, procedures, and processes can be found. As you compare the data on benchmarking items against your item, you may find that you are the best (world class), the same, or worse. If you are the best, congratulations. If your comparison is negative or the same, an opportunity exists to improve by studying another organization's or location's item.

Two types of data collected and used in the benchmarking process include qualitative data (word descriptions) and quantitative data (numbers, ratios, and so on). There has been much debate over which to collect first, and how to use each type of data. In reality, your benchmarking strategy should be designed to collect both types of data as opportunities present themselves. A quantitative data matrix should be developed and filled out during the data collection cycle. This matrix should highlight the parts of the process requiring additional data and study. It is best to complete the matrix as thoroughly as possible before doing surveys or visiting organizations (see Table 4-1).

Qualitative data also should be collected and analyzed. Some effective ways to present and analyze qualitative data are:

- Word charts (Table 4-2)
- Work word flowcharts (Table 4-3)
- Comparable process flowcharts (Fig. 4-1)

Do not be misled by the measurement data. Just because a location or an organization has better overall performance does not mean that all the activities within its process are world class. Every item has its strong and weak points. Use

TABLE 4-1   Data Matrix for New Hiring Process Benchmark

	COMPANY			
	A	B	C	OURS
Average days to bring new employees on board	45	65	20	45
Number of approvals required	5	5	2	4
Percentage of new employees who leave in first 12 months because of unsatisfactory performance	10	8	5	12
Wages compared with the average	1:1	0.8:1	1.1:1	1.1:1

TABLE 4-2   **Word Chart for the Hiring Process**

	COMPANY			
	A	B	C	OURS
Forms	One form for new hire and budget change	Four forms for budget, internal hire, external hire, and offer	Computers process all data; different screens used for budget and hiring	Two forms: one for budget, one for hiring
Budget change approval	2nd level	2nd level	2nd level	2nd level
	3rd level	3rd level	Accounting manager	3rd level
	Controller	Controller		Accounting manager
	Accounting manager	Accounting manager		
		Division VP		
New employee hiring approval	2nd level	2nd level	2nd level	2nd level
	3rd level	3rd level	Personnel manager	3rd level
	Plant manager	Plant manager		Industrial engineering
	Division personnel	Corporate personnel		Personnel manager
	Industrial engineering	Personnel manager		

all the data you have collected to search out the very best of each part of the item being studied. Frequently, the world's best organization does not have all the best individual parts of the item being studied, and input from organizations that

TABLE 4-3 Qualitative Work Word Flowchart

PROCESS USED BY A MANAGER TO START THE HIRING CYCLE

1. Check to see what the overtime has been for the last 3 months. Can get approval for a new hire if overtime in the department has been greater than 60 hours/week for the last 3 months.

2. Prepare job description for new employee.

3. Have salary administration evaluate the new job and classify it.

4. Prepare a payback analysis.

5. Fill out a personnel requisition form and obtain signoffs for next two levels.

6. If added budget is required, fill out a budget variation request and get next-level approval.

7. Prepare a letter of justification and send it to the controller for approval.

8. Send approved personnel request, budget variation request, and job description to personnel placement.

are not quite as good can give your organization the competitive advantage it is looking for. What the benchmarking organization needs to do is to select the best parts of each benchmarking partner's item and put them together to design a future-state solution that is better than any one of the individual items that were benchmarked.

Often, you will find that no one organization has all the right answers, and it will be necessary to combine activities from the organizations studied to establish a new best item. Combining the best elements from different benchmarking partners allows you to develop a new standard of excellence, and to become the benchmark organization for your item.

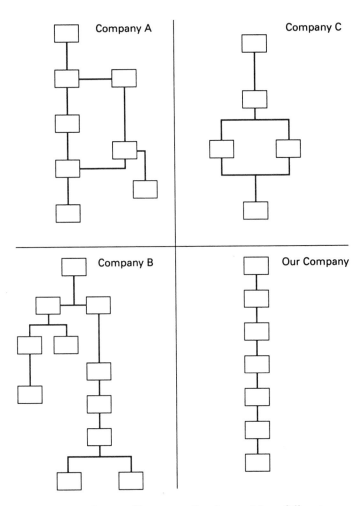

Figure 4-1. *Comparable process flowcharts of four different companies.*

It is a good idea to have the measurement chart updated to reflect all the surveys conducted, and all the data collected from other sources, before you visit an organization.

Having this information in hand pinpoints activities in the process with the greatest potential for a major breakthrough at your organization. The primary purpose of these visits is to observe activities firsthand, and to collect detailed qualitative data about planned-for or projected improvements to the item. The information collected not only should provide you with a picture of the current gap between you and the benchmarking partner; it should also furnish you with some insights into the benchmarking partner's item's past and future performance. It is essential to use this information to project where the world-class standard will be in the future. Change takes time, and even the best item must continue to improve. That is how it got to be the best.

The most dramatic and effective way to illustrate the difference between your item and the benchmarking partner's item is by a performance projection chart, often called a gap/trend analysis chart (see Fig. 4-2).

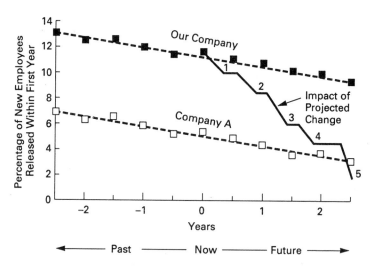

Figure 4-2. *Performance projection chart.*

In this chart, the *now* points are fixed by collected data. You can obtain your organization's past performance data by consulting its history file. Most organizations have registered some performance improvement over the years as a result of normal goal setting. Improvement in productivity of 2 to 5 percent per year is commonplace. If it is using a continuous improvement process, your organization should be improving at a rate of 10 to 20 percent a year without benchmarking. Using the established trend, the benchmarking item team (BIT) can project how the item will be performing over the next 3 years.

Additional consideration should be given to any planned-for improvement in the item's performance over the same 3-year period. If no data are available from the benchmarking partner, substitute your organization's slope for that of the benchmarking organization. If your item's projected improvement slope is greater than 10 percent a year, adopt the same slope in projecting the competitive item's performance. If your item's projected improvement is less than 10 percent, use 10 percent for the benchmarking partner's item until you can get better data. This substitute approach frequently provides very optimistic projections.

Normally, the best-of-breed organizations got there because their improvement rate was much better than that of other organizations. Analyzing each key measurement will reveal one of the following:

1. The gap is in favor of your organization.

2. There is no gap between your organization and the benchmark organization.

3. The gap is not in favor of your organization because
   • The gap is staying the same.
   • The gap is widening when your item is performing worse.

- The gap is narrowing when your item is performing better.

When there is no gap or the gap is unfavorable, the performance point is a candidate for an improvement action plan.

The gap/trend analysis chart can also be useful to help predict how effective potential improvements will be at reducing negative gaps. Figure 4.2 shows the projected impact on the item's performance over time when five separate improvements (numbers 1 through 5 on the graph) are implemented in the BIT's item.

SET TARGETS AND DEVELOP ACTION PLANS

When you start setting targets and developing action plans, qualitative information becomes invaluable, since it tells you what to do to bring about positive change. Many organizations try to implement all the beneficial activities and process changes they have discovered in one massive effort to make a step-function improvement in their item. This approach frequently has disastrous effects on the item. Some changes do not work, and bring the process to a standstill. Others have no impact, either positive or negative. But all of them cost something to implement and most of them add cost to the item.

At this stage, you have a lot of information in your hands. Proceed with caution. Prioritize the potential changes. Use a simulation computer model to prove out the proposed future-state solution before changes are implemented. Then pilot each change and measure the results. If the results are positive, implement the change and measure the effects of the completed implementation. If the results show a negative impact or no improvement, eliminate the change and proceed with the next change (see Fig. 4-3).

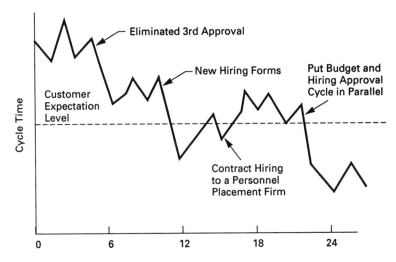

Figure 4-3. *Impact of change on the hiring process.*

TABLE **4-4** **Change Impact Analysis**

| | MEASUREMENT | | | | | |
CHANGE	A	B	C	D	E	COST TO IMPLEMENT
1	+5	N/A	+2	N/A	N/A	$30,000
2	N/A	+6	N/A	−1	N/A	20,000
3	+1	+3	N/A	+5	+1	500
4	−3	+1	N/A	N/A	+6	1,000
5	N/A	N/A	+6	N/A	N/A	1,000

N/A = not applicable.

The best way to prioritize your change activities is to prepare a change impact analysis (see Table 4-4). In this analysis, each of the key measurements you hope to improve is listed horizontally, and each of the proposed changes is listed vertically. The estimated impact in percentage or actual value that the proposed change will have on the measurement is recorded directly below the measurement. (Be sure that the unit of measurement—percentage or actual value— is constant so the figures can be summed.)

The change analysis must consider the total impact of the change. Many changes interact to impact more than one measurement. Often, a change may have a positive impact on one measurement but a negative impact on others. For example, reducing the density of an epoxy to make it easier to apply also might reduce the strength of the bond, causing the product to fail in the customer's application. Record the estimated cost to implement the change at the far right side of the projected activity line.

Using this analysis as a base, you can prioritize changes and assess their impact. Then prepare a performance projection chart to predict the impact of implementing priority changes. Adding the projected performance for the priority changes to the performance projection chart will help determine when and if your item will become world class (see Fig. 4-2).

DETERMINE BEST-VALUE FUTURE-STATE SOLUTION

Most benchmarking projects will provide the benchmarking item team with many different combinations of future-state solutions. The major mistake made by experienced and inexperienced BITs alike is to define a solution that provides the maximum positive change in the item's key measurements without considering other alternatives. For example, a team that is benchmarking the new product development process usually focuses on minimizing cycle time (a secondary measurement) without considering the primary measurement and its impact upon profit.

The profit impact of the new product development cycle is driven by increased market share and cost per development cycle. It is easy to see that there is an optimum operating point between increased market share and cost per development cycle that defines the best-value cycle time. For example, if an original cycle time of 3 years is reduced to 6 months for a product whose life cycle is 12 months, the organization may have a major problem on its hands. As a side effect, the organization has created some major peaks and valleys in the people resource requirements for new product development. It may be much better for the organization to have an 11-month development cycle if it can reduce the cost per cycle, because the shorter cycle is not viewed as value added to the customer.

Generally, at least three different potential future-state solutions should be prepared and evaluated to determine the best-value solution for the item. I am surprised at how often the best-value solution is not the one that maximizes the item's secondary measurements.

Update the Benchmark Item's Database

Benchmarking is a process of continuous discovery. As soon as you stop adding information to the database, it becomes out of date. Public domain data should be added to the database regularly, and someone should be assigned to review these new inputs to identify specific breakthroughs. Every 5 to 8 years, the total benchmarking process should be repeated. This is absolutely necessary. In today's high-technology world, key items are changing very rapidly. A simple technological breakthrough could revitalize an organization's item, and bring a dark horse up into first place overnight.

ORGANIZING FOR BENCHMARKING

BENCHMARKING'S RELATIONSHIP TO THE BUSINESS PLAN

Benchmarking is a lot like eating just one potato chip. I dare you to benchmark only one item and no more. Once an organization starts to benchmark, the process quickly becomes habit forming. It's similar to Amway's marketing strategy. If you benchmark one item and attain information from 10 other organizations, your organization is morally obligated to reciprocate with the 10 benchmarking partners when they want to benchmark one of their items. This could easily mean that you would be engaged in accumulating benchmarking data on 10 other items within a year.

This is not all bad, because benchmarking should be a key input into the organization's strategic plan and each year's business plan. Figure 5-1 shows the relationships among the elements of a strategic plan. The planning pyramid contains six interrelated levels.

1. *Mission.* The stated reason for the existence of the organization is its mission. The mission does not change frequently. Usually, it changes only when the organization decides to pursue a completely new market.

Figure 5-1. *The strategic planning pyramid.* (From H. J. Harrington, *The Improvement Process,* McGraw-Hill, 1987, p. 183.)

2. *Operating principles.* Operating principles are the basic beliefs that make up the culture of the organization. These principles rarely change.

3. *Business objectives.* Business objectives set the direction that the organization will follow for the next 10 to 20 years. (Example: "Increase the organization's market share in flexible-cable product lines.") Business objectives support the organization's mission.

4. *Performance goals.* Performance goals normally are quantified, measurable results that the organization wants to accomplish in a set period of time to support its business objectives. (Example: "Increase sales at a minimum rate of 12 percent a year from 1995 to 2005, with an average annual growth rate of 13 percent.") Performance goals relate directly to the business objectives.

5. *Strategies.* The strategies define the way the organization's performance goals will be accomplished. (Example: "The organization will identify new customer markets within the United States and concentrate on expanding new markets in the Pacific Rim countries.")

6. *Tactics.* The tactical plan defines the way the organization's strategy will be accomplished. Normally, tactics are specific tasks that will be undertaken in the short term (1 to 3 years) to move the organization toward the performance goals. (Example: "Sales offices will be opened in Tokyo, Beijing, Hong Kong, and Singapore within the next 12 months, and a customer-needs survey will be conducted in the surrounding areas to define new product needs.")

It is easy to understand how best-practices and future-trend information, gathered through benchmarking, has a major impact on the organization's mission, operating principles, business objectives, and performance goals. The results of the benchmarking projects are reflected in the future-state solutions that will also impact the organization's strategies and tactics.

The annual business plan that reflects the implementation of the organization's strategies and tactics must also reflect the implementation plans for future-state solutions, as well as the resources to do benchmarking projects for the coming year. Because of the major emphasis that most organizations are placing on breakthrough methodologies, it is very important that benchmarking projects be included in today's business plans. Benchmarking is one of the three key tools used in breakthrough methodologies. The other two are process redesign and process reengineering.

With the potential impact that benchmarking can have on the organization, it is imperative that the benchmarking process be understood and aggressively supported by top management if the process is to succeed. When talking about benchmarking, Kay R. Whitmore—chairman, president, and CEO of the Eastman Kodak Company—stated, "We are changing the way in which we work—no longer settling for incremental change when real breakthrough is required." Whitmore demonstrates his commitment to benchmarking by talking about it at regularly scheduled town meetings. He also personally served as a facilitator at the Benchmarking Business Roundtable. Benchmarking has been part of Eastman Kodak's improvement strategy since 1989.

BENCHMARKING'S SUPPORT STRUCTURE

It is foolhardy to believe that benchmarking can be embraced within a large or average-size organization without an organizational structure in place to support this key activity. The following are major players in a large organization's benchmarking structure:

- Executive Improvement Team
- Corporate Benchmarking Initiation Team or Corporate Benchmarking Steering Committee
- Corporate Vice President or Director of Corporate Benchmarking
- Corporate Benchmarking Office
- Benchmarking Site and/or Division Coordinators
- Site and/or Division Benchmarking Initiation Team or Benchmarking Steering Committee
- Benchmarking Item Team
- Benchmarking Item Team Facilitator

- Benchmarking Item Team Sponsor
- Internal Benchmarking Item Committee or Network

Figure 5-2 presents a typical benchmarking structure for a large corporation.

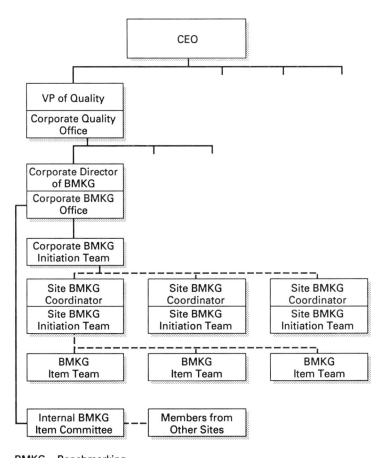

BMKG = Benchmarking

Figure 5-2. *Typical Benchmarking Organizational Matrix for a Large Corporation.*

Executive Improvement Team
(Top Management)

Most successful benchmarking programs are part of a *total improvement management* or *total quality management* strategy. These strategies include such activities as team building, statistical process control, activity-based costing, and quality policy deployment. These total improvement management processes are usually directed by an executive improvement team made up of the top management within the organization and chaired by the highest-ranking officer. As Edward Tracy, vice president of AT&T's MMS Division, put it: "If AT&T had not been into quality, I'm not sure we could have pulled off benchmarking because of the culture that it needs."

The benchmarking process should be part of the total improvement effort that the organization is engaged in, and as such should receive its direction and control from the executive improvement team. Organizations that do not have an existing executive improvement team to oversee improvement efforts should use this opportunity to form one to guide the benchmarking process.

CORPORATE BENCHMARKING INITIATION TEAM

The initiation team—sometimes called the corporate benchmarking steering committee or the corporate benchmarking cooperation committee—is a small group of people, usually from different divisions and/or sites, who are assigned to get the benchmarking process started, coordinate its implementation, and serve as in-house consultants for the benchmarking activities. For example, at IBM a group of eight experienced benchmarking experts was assembled as the benchmarking steering committee. The initiation team is responsible for:

- Avoiding duplication of efforts within the organization
- Communicating benchmarking findings and results
- Developing the organization's benchmarking process
- Standardizing benchmarking terminology
- Serving as the corporate contact point to outside organizations that want to benchmark
- Serving as a benchmarking resource to the total organization
- Developing standard benchmarking training packages
- Promoting benchmarking as an effective improvement tool
- Establishing a benchmarking code of conduct (code of ethics)
- Developing a corporate benchmarking database
- Preparing a central repository for benchmarking information and results
- Evaluating new benchmarking tools
- Defining benchmarking opportunities for the executive improvement team
- Coordinating the total organization's benchmarking activities
- Developing the corporate documentation that supports the benchmarking process (benchmarking management guide, necessary policy statements, checklists, benchmarking strategy, legal constraints, special benchmarking limitations, benchmarking rules, and so on)
- Integrating benchmarking projects into the organization's strategies and business plan
- Selling the value of benchmarking to management on an ongoing basis

- Serving as the organization's center of competence for benchmarking
- Developing the reward-and-recognition structure to support benchmarking
- Ensuring that benchmarks are recalibrated at regular intervals

Corporate Vice President or Director of Corporate Benchmarking

Often the benchmarking champion or czar is part of the quality-improvement organization. For example, at Eastman Kodak the director of corporate quality, vice president Ronald L. Heidke, reports to the CEO and president, Kay R. Whitmore. A. Turk Enustun, the director of corporate benchmarking, reports to Heidke. At IBM, the corporate responsibilities for support of the benchmarking strategy were assigned to the senior vice president of Market-Driven Quality. At Digital Equipment Corporation, coordination of benchmarking activities was assigned to Frank McCabe, corporate vice president of quality. Although some organizations have assigned responsibilities for coordination of benchmarking activities to a vice president of benchmarking, most organizations have avoided confusion and put benchmarking activities under the quality organization.

The director of corporate benchmarking is responsible for

- Serving as champion of the corporate benchmarking process
- Managing the corporate benchmarking office
- Being the prime benchmarking contact for outside organizations

- Ensuring that a standard benchmarking strategy is used throughout the organization
- Minimizing duplication of benchmarking activities
- Ensuring that a maximum return on investment is realized from benchmarking activities
- Coordinating site and/or divisional benchmarking activities
- Providing a focal point for benchmarking education
- Staying aware of late-breaking benchmarking developments so they can be implemented by the organization

Corporate Benchmarking Office

The corporate benchmarking office is a small team managed by the director of corporate benchmarking. For example, at Digital Equipment Corporation the corporate benchmarking office consists of three individuals: the director, a consultant, and an assistant. The corporate benchmarking office is responsible for:

- Increasing the level of sharing and communication on benchmarking activities
- Providing a point of contact for outside organizations
- Registering benchmarking item teams
- Reducing redundancies
- Coordinating corporate benchmarking activities
- Establishing and coordinating the corporate benchmarking database
- Helping define internal and external benchmarking partners
- Establishing benchmarking computer networks (examples: Eastman Kodak's network, called EKBENCH, became

available worldwide in June 1992; IBM's benchmarking network is called MDQBMARK FORUM)

- Helping identify high-potential opportunities
- Representing the corporation to outside benchmarking clearinghouses
- Maintaining the benchmarking training program
- Benchmarking the benchmarking process
- Assuring that site and/or division champions are assigned and operating effectively
- Preparing and maintaining the corporate benchmarking guide

Typical items included in the corporate guide are the benchmarking strategy, benchmarking process map, training requirements, key internal benchmarking contacts, requirements to register a benchmarking item team, the corporate code of ethics, legal requirements, lists of benchmark items that have completed the benchmarking cycle and/or are in the process, and literature research firms approved by the organization.

Benchmarking Site and/or Division Coordinators

Each site and/or division should have an individual assigned as its benchmarking champion. This individual plays a key role, serving as the site and/or division mentor for the benchmarking process. Site coordinators should be selected carefully. They need to be very experienced in the benchmarking process and have a high degree of motivation to make the process a success at the related site and/or division.

All lines of the business and geographic locations where the benchmarking process will be deployed should assign an individual to serve as benchmarking coordinator. The site benchmarking coordinators also usually serve as members of the corporate benchmarking initiation team. They function together, providing an internal network that coordinates the benchmarking activities throughout the organization. They will also very often chair a site and/or division benchmarking initiation team (steering committee), as described below. For example, in 1990 Gerald J. Balm was assigned as the benchmarking focal point (site coordinator) for IBM Rochester.

The site and/or division benchmarking coordinators are responsible for

- Serving on the corporate benchmarking initiation team
- Chairing the site and/or division benchmarking initiation team
- Coordinating the site and/or division benchmarking activities
- Serving as benchmarking consultants for the site and/or division
- Providing benchmarking training
- Identifying benchmarking opportunities
- Keeping management interested in the benchmarking process
- Highlighting benchmarking accomplishments
- Keeping the corporate benchmarking database updated
- Being a benchmarking advocate at the site and/or division
- Ensuring that benchmarking is done in a professional manner
- Ensuring that benchmarking rules are followed
- Serving as a benchmarking facilitator
- Providing the interface for the site and/or division to the corporate benchmarking office

- Ensuring that appropriate customer interface personnel are advised of pending benchmarking activities
- Evaluating incoming and outgoing benchmarking requests for applicability
- Being the site and/or division benchmarking center of competence
- Providing on-site consulting services
- Establishing an interface with local literature research firms
- Following the site and/or division's benchmarking activities to ensure that they are completed expeditiously
- Breaking down roadblocks encountered by benchmarking item teams
- Ensuring that cross-functional information is shared to minimize duplication
- Reviewing the makeup of benchmarking item teams
- Ensuring that all ethical, protocol, and legal guidelines are followed
- Maintaining outside connections to help with the benchmarking process

Site and/or Division Benchmarking Initiation Team (Steering Committee)

Typically, a small group of people, usually from different functions, are assigned to get the benchmarking process started, coordinate its implementation, and serve as consultants for the benchmarking activities within an individual division or at an individual site. This team is normally chaired by the benchmarking site and/or division coordinator. The team is made up of middle-level managers representing each of the functions within the organization. The site and/or division benchmarking initiation team is responsible for

- Conducting a business analysis and prioritizing benchmarking opportunities
- Ensuring that the benchmarking activities are reflected in the strategic plans and the yearly operating plan for the site and/or division
- Registering benchmarking item teams
- Standardizing the implementation of the benchmarking process within the organization
- Communicating benchmarking accomplishments
- Conducting post-mortems of benchmarking projects to improve future projects
- Coordinating activities within the site and/or division to eliminate or reduce duplication
- Promoting benchmarking within each function
- Ensuring that benchmarking becomes part of each middle manager's performance evaluation
- Ensuring that all individuals participating in the benchmarking process have been trained appropriately

Benchmarking Item Team (BIT)

The benchmarking item team (sometimes called the benchmarking team) usually consists of 5 to 10 people who are assigned to benchmark a specific business process, piece of equipment, product, or manufacturing process. (In some organizations the BIT may be as small as one person, assigned to handle all the different team roles.) A great deal of care should be taken in selecting the members of the benchmarking item team, because the success of the benchmarking study will depend upon the skills and creativity of the individuals who make up the team. Benchmarking item team members should have the following characteristics and/or knowledge:

- Good interpersonal skills—first impressions are very important in benchmarking
- Good understanding of the benchmarking process
- Good communication skills
- Excellent technical knowledge of the item being benchmarked
- The respect of people in the area where the change will occur
- Knowledge of Organizational Change Management methodologies
- Skill in dealing with consultants and/or outside organizations
- The ability to influence others
- A high degree of top management credibility
- The ability to embrace change as a way of life
- The ability to sell and implement the benchmarking findings
- High interest in the project
- A high degree of creativity, innovativeness, and flexibility
- Enough time to take on the assignment

In addition, a BIT member could be the process owner, the best representative from his or her department, and/or a customer of the item. It is sometimes beneficial to have a customer on the benchmarking item team.

The benchmarking item team will operate for 6 to 18 months, depending on what is being benchmarked and the type of benchmarking approach that is used. A typical team is made up of:

- A team leader
- A number of content and/or process experts
- A person (not part of the present process) who can give an objective view of the benchmark item's performance
- A data analyst
- Key people who will be needed to help implement the future-state solution developed by the benchmarking item team
- A facilitator who helps the team leader and the team stay on track and use the proper tools

The benchmarking item team has seven key responsibilities:

1. Develop the benchmark item's project plan.
2. Define the benchmark item's critical measurements.
3. Collect and analyze data about and from the benchmarking partners.
4. Develop a future-state solution.
5. Sell management on the advantages of implementing the future-state solution.
6. Assist with implementation of the future-state solution.
7. Perform periodic reviews of the benchmark item's database after the future-state solution is implemented.

Typically, members of the benchmarking item team will spend 15 to 30 percent of their time on the benchmarking project—from project initiation to the point in the process where the future-state solution is accepted by upper management. The team leader will devote 25 to 40 percent of his or her time to the benchmarking project during this same period.

Benchmarking Item Team Facilitator

A trained, experienced facilitator who is not involved with the item under study should be assigned to each benchmarking item team until the benchmarking process becomes internalized into the organization.

The BIT facilitator plays a key role in the way the benchmarking item team functions. A facilitator must have an excellent understanding of the benchmarking and team processes, although he or she needs little if any knowledge of the benchmark item. The BIT facilitator is responsible for working with the team leader to

- Establish team agendas
- Define team roles
- Obtain agreements
- Define leader and team weaknesses and how to correct them
- Develop the Organizational Change Management plan
- Obtain team ownership of the future-state solution
- Enforce agreements
- Keep meetings on track, following the agenda and focusing on outcomes
- Create a win-win outcome when disagreements arise

The BIT facilitator is often called upon to provide the benchmarking item team with just-in-time training related to the benchmarking process. This individual should possess the following key characteristics:

- Stays neutral
- Behaves in a positive way
- Is a good listener
- Is not defensive
- Encourages the team when things are not going well
- Reacts quickly to body language
- Talks only when necessary
- Is not afraid to interrupt the team when it is going off course
- Can criticize without hurting feelings

Benchmarking Item Team Sponsor

A benchmarking item team sponsor is frequently assigned to a BIT that is working on improving a critical business item. The sponsor is usually a very high-level person (typically a director or vice president) who cannot commit the required time to be the chairperson of or participate in the specific BIT, but is very interested in seeing that the project meets its goals. Often the BIT chair will report directly to the benchmarking item team sponsor through the established structure. The BIT sponsor will

- Regularly review the BIT's progress
- Break down roadblocks that cannot be handled by the BIT
- Serve as adviser to the BIT on the item being benchmarked
- Help keep the BIT's resources intact

Internal Benchmarking Item Committee or Network

The internal benchmarking item committee is made up of representatives from different sites and/or divisions who have a common interest in benchmarking a specific item. By combining their resources, they can accomplish the benchmarking project using fewer individual resources than would be required if independent studies were made. In addition, internal benchmarking item committees usually develop future-state solutions that have a better fit between sites and/or divisions than would be developed if the individual future-state solutions were developed independently. The responsibilities of the internal benchmarking item committee parallel those of the benchmarking item team.

THE FIVE PHASES OF THE BENCHMARKING PROCESS

This book is intended to help the reader and his or her organization effectively implement benchmarking into the total organization. It will cover the five phases of the benchmarking process (see Fig. 6-1). These phases, in order of coverage, are:

Phase I	Planning the Benchmarking Process and Characterization of the Item(s)
Phase II	Internal Data Collection and Analysis
Phase III	External Data Collection and Analysis
Phase IV	Improvement of the Item's Performance
Phase V	Continuous Improvement

These benchmarking phases comprise a total of 20 activities (see Table 6-1). Each activity is subdivided into a number of specific tasks (see Fig. 6-2).*

---

*A total of 144 tasks are discussed in *The Complete Benchmarking Implementation Guide* (McGraw-Hill, 1996).

Become a Star Using Benchmarking

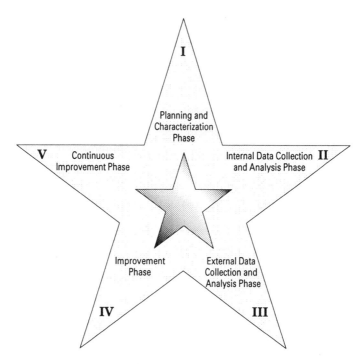

Figure 6-1. *The five phases of the benchmarking process.*

PHASE I: PLANNING THE BENCHMARKING PROCESS AND CHARACTERIZATION OF THE ITEM(S)

The planning phase entails defining important issues that are necessary for directing the benchmarking activities into the most desirable and profitable areas for the individual and/or organization. Detailed, specific measurement approaches are then developed to formulate the plans necessary to carry out the benchmarking process.

TABLE 6-1   The 5 Phases and 20 Activities of the Benchmarking
Process

BENCHMARKING PHASE	RELATED ACTIVITIES
Phase I Planning the Benchmarking Process and Characterization of the Item(s)	1. Identify what to benchmark 2. Obtain top management support 3. Develop the measurement plan 4. Develop the data collection plan 5. Review the plans with location experts 6. Characterize the benchmark item
Phase II Internal Data Collection and Analysis	7. Collect and analyze internal published information 8. Select potential internal benchmarking sites 9. Collect internal original research information 10. Conduct interviews and surveys 11. Form an internal benchmarking committee 12. Conduct internal site visits
Phase III External Data Collection and Analysis	13. Collect external published information 14. Collect external original research information
Phase IV Improvement of the Item's Performance	15. Identify corrective actions 16. Develop an implementation plan 17. Gain top management approval of the future-state solution 18. Implement the future-state solution and measure its impact
Phase V Continuous Improvement	19. Maintain the benchmarking database 20. Implement continuous performance improvement

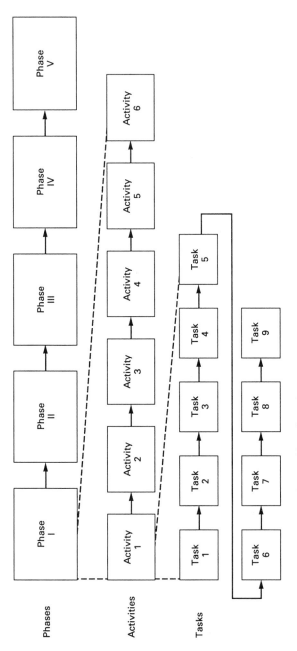

Figure 6-2. *Hierarchy for the total benchmarking management process.*

ACTIVITY 1—IDENTIFY WHAT TO BENCHMARK

The first step in the benchmarking process is the formation of the benchmarking initiation team (BT). This team is comprised of individuals who accept the responsibility to start and manage the entire benchmarking process. In many large organizations, the BT becomes a department that provides support for all the benchmarking studies.

Once a BT is formed, it must clearly identify exactly what needs to be benchmarked. This seems to be an obvious and logical starting point for the benchmarking initiation team, since all other decisions will stem from it. Nonetheless, many organizations fail to nail down exactly what they are trying to do before they actually do it. A more frequent approach is for an executive to announce that benchmarking is good and the organization should be doing it. General management is then left to carry the ball from there. It is easy to see why this approach is wrong and how it can cost the organization a lot of time and money.

In identifying what to benchmark, the BT will be choosing among four categories:

- Business processes
- Equipment
- Manufacturing (production) processes
- Products and services

In this activity, you also need to cover what the benchmarking initiation team should do if it is not sure which category to benchmark. Here BT members will need to conduct a complete business analysis that requires them to thoroughly understand the organization's business plan, yearly performance results, critical success factors, and core assets (core capabilities and core competencies). Then they will need to perform a competitive analysis related to the key products and core assets. Once the analysis is complete, the benchmarking initiation team must analyze the data to determine how the benchmarking resources should be deployed to support the organization's performance measurements and planned-for activities. (For example, part of the 3-year plan might be to install a new, computerized order-entry process. If so, equipment benchmarking would be a priority to support this project.) Once the appropriate category has been selected, the BT must learn how to select the specific item to be benchmarked.

Following is a list of the tasks completed during Activity 1:

- A benchmarking initiation team was formed.
- A list of critical success factors for the organization was reviewed or prepared.
- A competitive analysis was completed.
- Core assets (core capabilities and competencies) were reviewed or defined.
- The organization's business plan was reviewed to define its impact on the benchmarking process.
- The benchmarking categories of importance to the organization were defined and prioritized.
- Specific items to be benchmarked were defined and prioritized.
- The items were defined and characterized for benchmarking internally and/or externally.

ACTIVITY 2—OBTAIN TOP MANAGEMENT (EXECUTIVE TEAM) SUPPORT

After defining what it is you wish to benchmark, you need to obtain top management's support of the items to be benchmarked and a formal benchmarking structure. Benchmarking, done properly, needs the commitment of the organization's top management, so that adequate time and resources will be made available for the project. Most important, you want to get support for implementation of the changes that will be recommended as a result of the benchmarking process.

In order to receive this support, you need to build understanding not only about what benchmarking is but also about how it can help an organization. In the end, you will create and present a benchmarking proposal to top management. The proposal will include:

- The detailed benchmarking process that will be used
- The formal organizational structure required to support the benchmarking activities
- A code of conduct (ethics)
- A 3-year plan of categories and items per category to be benchmarked
- A list of near-term items to be benchmarked
- A return-on-investment analysis

Also during this activity, the organization's executives will be trained in the use of the benchmarking process. If top management approves the benchmarking project and funds it, benchmarking item teams (BITs) will be formed to conduct the required evaluations.

Following is a list of the tasks completed during Activity 2:

- The benchmarking item team(s) was formed.
- A benchmarking process and strategy were prepared and approved by top management.
- A 3-year benchmarking project plan was prepared and approved.

- A benchmarking organizational structure was defined and approved.
- A standard list of terms and definitions was developed.
- A benchmarking training program was established and implemented.
- A list of benchmarking support tools was defined, and training programs were developed for each tool.
- A benchmarking code of ethics was developed.
- The proposed benchmark items were reviewed to define how improving them would affect the organization's primary performance measurements. This analysis was used to prioritize the benchmark items.
- Proposals were prepared and approved to support the benchmarking of individual items.
- Resources were set aside for the benchmarking efforts.
- The pros and cons of outside consultants were discussed and a decision was made on using them. If the organization decided to go ahead, the consultants were selected.
- The item's benchmarking plan and project file were established.

ACTIVITY 3—DEVELOP THE MEASUREMENT PLAN

In this activity, you will ask, "What are the characteristics of the benchmark item? Which characteristics are candidates for improvement? What am I going to measure, and how am I going to measure it?" By establishing measurements, you are, in fact, preparing to compare your benchmark item with a similar item. The accuracy and consistency of your benchmarking study are highly dependent on how well this activity is performed.

Following is a list of the tasks completed during Activity 3:

- The BIT was trained on different types of measurement approaches.
- A fishbone diagram was prepared for each primary measurement.
- The benchmark item's measurement characteristics were defined.
- Measurement charts were developed.
- The item's measurement procedures were completed.

ACTIVITY 4—DEVELOP THE DATA COLLECTION PLAN

In some benchmarking studies, it is imperative to collect information from both internal (inside the organization) and external (outside the organization) sources. There are four sources from which you can collect data for your benchmark item. The data collection plan will include:

1. Information about how the item is performing at other locations and/or sites within your organization (internal benchmarking):
   - Look for published information about internal organizations.
   - Collect nonpublished information (original research).
2. Information about how the item is performing at locations and/or sites external to the total organization (external benchmarking):
   - Look for published information about external organizations.
   - Collect nonpublished information (original research).

In this activity, you will determine how to prepare the right data collection plan for a particular benchmark item. You will also develop an initial list of potential benchmarking partners—internal and/or external organizations with items that are the same as or similar to your item and that may be performing better than your item. This list will be the start of your benchmarking plan.

Following is a list of the tasks completed during Activity 4:

- The data analysis methods were defined.
- A measurement procedure was developed.
- An item characterization plan was completed.
- A plan to collect internal information was developed.
- A plan to collect external information was developed.
- A list of potential benchmarking partners was developed.
- The item's benchmarking time-line chart was prepared.
- The item's benchmarking plan was expanded and detailed.
- The Organizational Change Management plan was created.

ACTIVITY 5—REVIEW THE PLANS WITH LOCATION EXPERTS

Location experts are individuals who understand the benchmark item, and can help you find sources of information related to it. In this activity, you will review the plans that you formulated in Activities 3 and 4 with location experts to gain their insight on the benchmarking process and identify further potential contacts. After this review, plans will be updated and revised to include the recommendations of the location experts.

Following is a list of the tasks completed during Activity 5:

- The benchmark item's location experts were identified.
- Meetings were held with location experts to discuss the data collection and benchmarking plans.

- The data collection and benchmarking plans were updated on the basis of input from the location experts.

- The Organizational Change Management plan was updated.

ACTIVITY 6—CHARACTERIZE THE BENCHMARK ITEM

In this activity, you will set up measurement systems and collect the data required to completely characterize your benchmark item. The collected information will be used to start your benchmark item database. Great care should be taken to ensure that the data collected are accurate, because the rest of the benchmarking process will use the data as a starting point.

Following is a list of the tasks completed during Activity 6:

- A characterization work plan was established.

- Employees were trained to collect the required data.

- The forms used to collect and analyze the data were designed.

- The benchmark item was characterized.

- The benchmark item's database was established.

- A measurement matrix was created.

- The early phases of the Organizational Change Management plan were implemented, and appropriate Organizational Change Management surveys were conducted.

PHASE II: INTERNAL DATA COLLECTION AND ANALYSIS

It is good practice to look within your organization to see how other departments, functions, divisions, and/or locations are using the benchmark item before you start contacting "external" organizations. Individuals reporting into the same management chain are more motivated to help and have fewer restrictions on the information they can exchange than do outside contacts. During Phase II, you will collect only information internal to the organization. The term *internal*, as used in benchmarking, refers to all organizations (corporations, conglomerates, governments, companies, and so on) within the same management structure.

ACTIVITY 7—COLLECT AND ANALYZE INTERNAL PUBLISHED INFORMATION

Having already defined what information needs to be collected (see Activity 4), you will now go about collecting that information. Internal published information most often takes the form of technical reports and studies published within the organization. But it is certainly not limited to those forms. For example, your organization may have had external articles or newspaper coverage on how it is using the benchmark item. This information will be used to update the database and identify potential internal benchmarking partners.

Following is a list of the tasks completed during Activity 7:

- A work plan to collect internal published information was developed.

- Publication sources that could contain information about the item's internal performance were identified.

- Copies of important published documents were collected and analyzed.

- The benchmarking database was updated to include summaries of the analyzed publications.

- The benchmarking plan and the internal potential benchmarking partners' list were updated.

ACTIVITY 8—SELECT POTENTIAL INTERNAL BENCHMARKING SITES

During this activity, you will select the internal benchmarking sites or partners that the BIT would like to exchange information with. Selecting internal benchmarking sites can be very beneficial, since you often get better control and cooperation from those inside your own organization than you do from outside sources. Another advantage is that you can exchange confidential information that outside organizations would be unwilling to share with you and/or would be legally prohibited from sharing with you.

The benchmarking item team (BIT)'s list of potential internal benchmarking partners has already been updated by the location experts (Activity 5) and revised as a result of collecting internal published information (Activity 7). In large organizations this list of potential internal benchmarking partners can be very long, and the BIT may want to limit its contact to the very best sites. The other side of the picture is that all potential benchmarking sites are likely to benefit from the benchmarking study and as such should participate. A useful approach is to divide the BIT's list into an A list and a B list. The A list defines the sites that the BIT wants to collect data from. The sites on this priority list should be given special incentives to become internal benchmarking partners. The sites on the B list should also be invited to participate in the benchmarking process. Once the potential internal benchmarking partners have been selected, the BIT should send an invitation letter explaining the details of the project and requesting that an individual be identified as the location interface to the BIT for this project.

Following is a list of the tasks completed during Activity 8:

- The potential internal benchmarking partner list was prioritized.
- A list of site contacts was prepared.

ACTIVITY 9—COLLECT INTERNAL ORIGINAL RESEARCH INFORMATION

Internal original research is any type of research that has not been previously published. This type of research is more difficult to collect, because it is not readily available, but it is useful and needed information—especially if the benchmark item is not a common item. Often, smaller items get bypassed by the published literature because there is not a large enough audience for the information. Knowing how to conduct original research is an art, but one that can be mastered. Activities 9, 10, and 11 are all designed to collect and analyze internal information and data (internal original research).

In order to get the internal original research activities started, the BIT should send copies of its measurement plan and its characterization data to each of the internal benchmarking partners' coordinators. The benchmarking partners should collect compatible data and input it into a central database. As the many inputs come in from the different benchmarking partners, the BIT will analyze the information and compare it with the BIT's item's data to identify negative gaps. For each negative gap, a gap/trend analysis chart will be prepared. Since each negative gap represents a potential improvement opportunity, a root cause/corrective action form is prepared for it as well. The BIT will also develop a clarification list for each internal benchmarking partner that defines what additional information is required.

At the same time that the BIT is analyzing the data and identifying improvement opportunities, each internal benchmarking partner will be performing similar tasks.

Following is a list of the tasks completed during Activity 9:

- All potential internal benchmarking partners were contacted and asked to become internal item benchmarking partners.
- A list of internal item benchmarking partners was completed.
- All internal item benchmarking partners assigned a site representative to work with the BIT.
- The benchmarking and measurement plans were updated on the basis of inputs from the internal item benchmarking partners.
- All internal benchmarking partners' items were characterized.
- A central database was established for the benchmark item.
- Gap/trend analysis charts were prepared by all sites.
- Each site established a root cause/corrective action list.

ACTIVITY 10—CONDUCT INTERNAL INTERVIEWS AND SURVEYS

At this point in the benchmarking process, the BIT begins to identify root causes and the appropriate corrective actions for the benchmarking measurements. A *root cause* is a specific reason that some other organization's benchmark item's performance is better than your benchmark item's performance. A *corrective action* is a strategy that details how you can use root cause information to improve your benchmark item. As additional information is obtained, the database is updated. By the end of this important activity, the root causes of all the negative gaps and most of the associated corrective actions should be defined.

Following is a list of the tasks completed during Activity 10:

- All internal benchmarking partners whose items were outperforming the BIT's item were contacted to understand why their items were performing better.
- Critical indicators in the measurement matrix were verified to be sure they were correct.
- Root causes were defined for all improvement opportunities.
- All root cause/corrective action combinations were classified.
- The benchmarking database was updated.

ACTIVITY 11—FORM AN INTERNAL BENCHMARKING COMMITTEE

For some benchmark items, it may be advisable to form an internal benchmarking committee made up of one person from each benchmarking site plus additional technical experts as needed. This is a committee that draws on the special talents and resources of other individuals working within the total organization (other locations and/or sites). The committee members will work together, sharing information so that each organization can benefit from the benchmarking process. An internal benchmarking committee is usually formed whenever external benchmarking is used to maximize the benefits from the external contact. In advanced benchmarking organizations, these committees are often formed during Activity 4 or 7.

Following is a list of the tasks completed during Activity 11:

- The BIT determined if there was sufficient interest in forming an internal benchmarking committee, made up of the benchmarking partners, for the item under study.
- If sufficient interest was defined, an internal benchmarking committee was formed.
- The internal benchmarking committee was trained in the benchmarking process.
- A set of responsibilities for the internal benchmarking committee was defined and a program plan was prepared.
- The internal benchmarking committee's plan was integrated into the total benchmarking plan.

ACTIVITY 12—CONDUCT INTERNAL SITE VISITS

Among the internal benchmarking sites that were chosen, there will be certain ones that you will need to visit. The site visit is conducted not to collect measurement data, but to define corrective actions. Activities 7–11 were designed to define performance improvement opportunities and the root causes of negative gaps. By this point in the process, most of the corrective actions related to each defined root cause probably have also been identified. The visit should be designed to allow the BIT to

1. Verify the difference between the site's item and the BIT's item
2. Understand why the benchmarking partner's item is performing better
3. Define how the benchmark item can be improved
4. Collect information about the resources required to implement corrective actions

The site visit should be well orchestrated. Agreed-to agendas must be prepared well in advance. Arrangements need to be made so that the visitation team will meet with people who can answer questions with factual information. There should be a good technical and intellectual balance between the visitation team members and the people they will be meeting with at the internal benchmarking partner's site.

The site visitation team should be made up of three to six people. One member should be assigned as spokesperson for the team, another as team scribe. Each team member should have a preassigned set of corrective actions that he or she will be collecting information about.

Here are some key site visitation points:

1. Show up a little early; never keep your host waiting.

2. Start the meeting by reviewing the agenda and agreeing on the people who will be involved in each agenda item.

3. Structure the meeting so that both the BIT and the internal benchmarking partner benefit from the exchange of information.

4. Be sure that the agenda includes time to tour the item's process and time for the visitation team to meet with people who are actually part of the process.

5. It is often better to divide the visitation team into smaller groups to investigate individual corrective actions.

6. Set aside time before the end of the site visit for members of the visitation team to meet together privately. The team can then summarize its findings and identify points that need additional research before it leaves the site.

7. At the end of the site visit, review the key findings with the host to be sure that there are no misunderstandings.

8. Within 24 hours of the site visit, the visitation team should meet to discuss and document its findings.

9. A copy of the trip report should be sent to the internal benchmarking partner's coordinator for review and comments before it is distributed.

Following is a list of the tasks completed during Activity 12:

• The benchmarking partner sites that need to be visited were identified.

• Agendas and lists of questions were customized for each site to be visited.

• Visitation team(s) were identified and trained, and made location visits.

• The root cause portion of the root cause/corrective action database was completed.

• At least one corrective action was defined for each root cause.

• The implementation part of the database was initiated.

• Trip reports were prepared for each site visit.

PHASE III: EXTERNAL DATA COLLECTION AND ANALYSIS

An external benchmarking partner is defined as an individual or organization that reports to a completely independent management chain. An example is IBM benchmarking with Hewlett-Packard, Ford Motor Company, and Toyota. This phase is designed to help the BIT collect and analyze data from potential and actual external benchmarking partners.

ACTIVITY 13—COLLECT EXTERNAL PUBLISHED INFORMATION

For most benchmarking studies, once the sources of externally published information relevant to a benchmark item have been identified, it is relatively easy to collect the data. Since the information is part of the public domain, and is therefore not proprietary, there is usually no difficulty in acquiring it. The difficult and time-consuming part of Activity 13 is analyzing the mountains of information available. The result of this analysis is a greatly expanded measurement database, and a list of potential benchmarking partners.

Following is a list of the tasks completed during Activity 13:

- The BIT developed a detailed external data collection plan.
- A work plan was developed to acquire relevant external published information.
- Appropriate databases were searched to develop a list of relevant articles, reports, and books.
- Copies of relevant publications were obtained, read, analyzed, and summarized.
- The benchmarking plan and the database were updated.

ACTIVITY 14—COLLECT EXTERNAL ORIGINAL RESEARCH INFORMATION

During this activity, the BIT's creativity takes on great prominence, because even though unpublished, nonconfidential external original research is available to the public, it can be very difficult to actually accumulate this information. Doing external original research is a lot like being a detective. The clues are all available, but the BIT has to be very creative in finding them and combining them so that it can identify the right organizations to contact to become benchmarking partners. By formulating a good data collection plan and dealing with knowledgeable location experts, you can lessen the difficulty of this activity and make the time you spend conducting such research as effective as possible.

Activity 14 is the most complex and, at the same time, one of the most rewarding activities in the benchmarking process. It is divided into seven subactivities, as shown in Fig. 6-3.

14A   Update the external original research part of the benchmarking plan.

14B   Collect data from external experts.

14C   Exchange information with external benchmarking partners.

14D   Survey external customers and potential customers.

14E   Conduct competitive shopping.

14F   Reverse-engineer competitive products.

14G   Update the benchmarking database and the root cause/corrective action list.

This one activity accounts for 36 of the 144 tasks that make up the benchmarking process.

The benchmark item will progress through a very different series of tasks, depending on the benchmarking category it falls into. All benchmarking categories will be processed through subactivities 14A and 14B. At that point, manufacturing processes, business processes, and equipment will continue through subactivity 14C. Competitive services will be processed through subactivities 14D and 14E. Competitive products will be processed through subactivities 14D and 14F. All products will go through subactivity 14G, at which point the results of the BIT's activities are used to update the

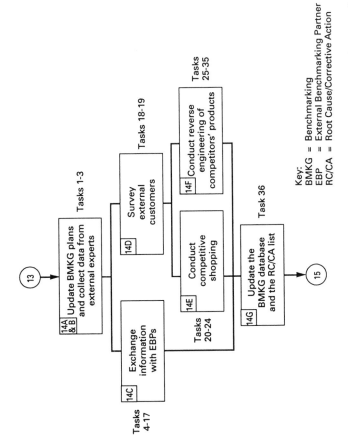

Figure 6-3. *Overview flow diagram of Activity 14—collect external original research information.*

benchmarking database and the root cause/corrective action list.

SUBACTIVITY 14A—UPDATE THE EXTERNAL ORIGINAL RESEARCH PART OF THE BENCHMARKING PLAN. Activity 14 starts by updating the external original research part of the benchmarking plan to reflect the many insights gained by the BIT in collecting external published information (Activity 13).

SUBACTIVITY 14B—COLLECT DATA FROM EXTERNAL EXPERTS. The BIT will implement the benchmarking plan by contacting external experts to gain more information about the item under study. Typical external experts that might be contacted include:

- Professional associations
- Consultants
- Independent testing firms
- Universities
- Company-watchers (brokerage firms)
- Software firms
- Research organizations

All contacts with these external experts should be well orchestrated. The BIT should know exactly why it is contacting each expert and have prepared a list of questions to be asked. Typical questions for external experts are:

- Which organizations are the best?
- Why are they the best?
- How good are they (actual performance measurements)?
- Who can we contact in the organization to gain more information?

- What are the latest advances related to the item under study?
- Who are the leading research organizations related to the item under study?

SUBACTIVITY 14C—EXCHANGE INFORMATION WITH EXTERNAL BENCHMARKING PARTNERS.   Information exchange is used for all items except competitive services and products. Once the potential external benchmarking partners have been identified, the BIT will begin to develop a cooperative relationship with these organizations. Typically, the cooperative relationship will develop along the following path:

1. Phone calls will be made to specific individuals at the potential benchmarking partner's site to explain the project and to get their agreement to participate.

2. Copies of the performance data for the BIT's item, along with a survey, will be sent directly to the external benchmarking partner's coordinator.

3. The BIT will analyze the data that is returned from the external benchmarking partner and prepare a list of additional questions that it would like to raise. The BIT will also perform a gap analysis at this time.

4. A conference call will be conducted with the external benchmarking partner to clarify any misunderstood data and to discuss negative gaps in the BIT's item. The purpose of this phone call is to clarify any questionable data, define root causes for all negative gaps, and identify potential corrective action(s).

5. The visitation team will visit the external benchmarking partner's site to gain a more detailed understanding of the benchmarking partner's item and to better define

what it would take to implement similar approaches into the BIT's item's process.

6. A final report comparing each external benchmarking partner with the total population and the BIT's future-state solution will be prepared, with a copy sent to each benchmarking partner.

SUBACTIVITY 14D—SURVEY EXTERNAL CUSTOMERS AND POTENTIAL CUSTOMERS.   Usually the BIT will not get the cooperation needed from competitors to conduct a competitive product or service benchmarking activity. This means that the BIT will have to generate the required data itself. Some of this information may already have been obtained from the external experts (Underwriters Laboratory, *Consumer Reports,* J. D. Powers, user groups, and so on). Usually independent analysis is still required. To start this effort, the BIT will need to survey external customers and potential customers of the item to define which of the measurements are most important to them, their perspective on how their own item compares with the BIT's item, and what they would like to see improved the most.

SUBACTIVITY 14E—CONDUCT COMPETITIVE SHOPPING.   If the BIT is benchmarking service, it will use the information obtained to design a competitive shopping program that will systematically collect the required comparison data. Competitive shopping should not be handled casually. The process should be well designed and documented, and the competitive shoppers must be well trained to obtain the desired results.

SUBACTIVITY 14F—REVERSE-ENGINEER COMPETITIVE PRODUCTS. If the BIT is focusing on benchmarking competitive products, it will periodically purchase products from competitors to test and disassemble along with a correlation sample of the BIT's product. Typical points to be analyzed include:

Order cycle time	Environmental performance
Packaging protection	Suppliers
Installation instructions	Ease of repair
Product characteristics	Assembly methods
Initial performance	Workmanship
Reliability	Cost to produce
Safety factors	

This procedure, although seemingly on the unethical side, is totally legal and is practiced by most organizations. Knowing what your competitors are doing often helps you leapfrog them, providing the organization with a major competitive advantage.

SUBACTIVITY 14G—UPDATE THE BENCHMARKING DATABASE AND THE ROOT CAUSE/CORRECTIVE ACTION LIST. The information collected in subactivities 14B–14F is now analyzed and added to the benchmarking database. At this point in the benchmarking process, all negative gaps should be understood, their root causes determined, and at least one potential corrective action defined for each root cause. In addition, a great deal of information has been collected about the amount of resources required to implement many of the potential corrective actions.

THE PURPOSE OF ACTIVITY 14. Activity 14 is designed to provide the BIT with the information necessary to define the root cause(s) of negative gaps in its item and to identify corrective actions that can eliminate these negative gaps.

Following is a list of the tasks completed during Activity 14:

- The external original research plan was updated.
- Data were collected from external experts.
- The list of external benchmarking partners was completed.
- A list of organizations that agreed to become benchmarking partners was prepared.
- A list of measurements that will be shared with the external benchmarking partners was developed.
- Focus group meetings were held with the external benchmarking partners.
- Surveys of the performance of external benchmarking partners' items were completed.
- Gap/trend analysis charts were prepared.
- A survey clarification list was prepared and discussed with the external benchmarking partners.
- A root cause/corrective action database was generated for each identified negative gap.
- Visits were made to the external partners' sites.
- Root causes for all improvement opportunities were identified and potential corrective actions were defined for some of them.
- External customer and potential customer surveys and focus group meetings were conducted.
- Competitive shopping evaluation procedures were developed.
- Competitive shoppers were trained.
- Competitive shopping evaluations were conducted.
- A list of competitors' competitive advantages was developed.
- Competitors' packaging and documentation were analyzed.

- The competitive item's performance reliability was compared with that of the BIT's item.
- The competitive products were reverse-engineered.
- The benchmarking database was updated.

PHASE IV: IMPROVEMENT OF THE ITEM'S PERFORMANCE

With benchmarking data on a particular item at hand, the BIT is now ready to enter the improvement phase. This phase defines not only how an item should be improved but also the steps necessary to implement these changes and to measure their effectiveness.

ACTIVITY 15—IDENTIFY CORRECTIVE ACTIONS

Once you have established a measurement database and understand why gaps exist between you and your benchmarking partners, you can evaluate different alternatives to identify best-value future-state solutions. In this activity, you will identify the appropriate corrective actions defined during the benchmarking process. Part of this activity will be a benefits/cost/risk analysis.

In most cases, the benchmarking item team will define a number of potential future-state solutions. Each of these potential solutions should be evaluated to determine the best-value future-state solution. To make this determination, the BIT needs to consider three questions:

- How much will the item's performance improve?
- How much will it cost and how long will it take to implement the future-state solution?

- What impact will the change have on each of the item's stakeholders?

Following is a list of the tasks completed during Activity 15:

- The BIT completed the list of potential corrective actions.
- The gap/trend analysis charts were updated to reflect the potential corrective actions.
- A measurement interaction chart was created.
- The corrective actions were prioritized.
- A group of potential future-state solution models was created and flowcharted.
- Simulation models were created and exercised for the high-potential future-state solutions.
- A benefits/cost/risk analysis was made of high-potential future-state solutions.
- The best-value future-state solution was defined.
- The benchmarking plan and database were updated.

ACTIVITY 16—DEVELOP AN IMPLEMENTATION PLAN

Having identified the best-value future-state solution, the BIT must set its sights on developing an implementation plan. Part of the implementation activity will involve designing an Organizational Change Management plan that will minimize resistance to change and prepare the organization to embrace the future-state solution.

Following is a list of the tasks completed during Activity 16:

- The preferred future-state solution and its supporting data were reviewed with the internal experts.
- The proposed implementation team was defined.

- The implementation plan was prepared.
- The Organizational Change Management plan that supports the future-state solution was developed.
- The implementation budget was prepared.

ACTIVITY 17—GAIN TOP MANAGEMENT APPROVAL OF THE FUTURE-STATE SOLUTION

Because of the impact most benchmarking projects have on the organization, top managers must be committed to the plan. They do not need to be directly involved in the detailed activities, but they must back the plan morally and financially. In Activity 17, the BIT will present its project report and preferred future-state solution to the appropriate upper-management levels for approval.

When the future-state solution is accepted by top management, a benchmarking implementation team (IT) will be assigned to complete the project.

Following is a list of the tasks completed during Activity 17:

- An item benchmarking project report was prepared.
- The item benchmarking project report was reviewed individually with each of the executives.
- The key executive's Organizational Change Management status was changed from a target to a sustaining sponsor or advocate.
- The future-state solution and its supporting budget were approved.
- A budget structure to support the implementation of the future-state solution was established.
- A customized final report on the project was sent to each benchmarking partner.

ACTIVITY 18—IMPLEMENT THE FUTURE-STATE SOLUTION AND MEASURE ITS IMPACT

Here is the moment of truth, the time to take all the theories and plans and see if they work in the real world—your world. If it has followed the benchmarking process carefully, the benchmarking implementation team, supported by technologists, will be in the best position to implement these changes to your business. It is often necessary to pilot complex changes before they are implemented. Changes should be implemented sequentially, so that each individual change can be measured independently. Care should be taken to ensure that changes to the benchmark item do not have a negative impact on other areas of the organization.

Following is a list of the tasks completed during Activity 18:

- An implementation team was formed.
- The implementation plan was updated.
- The Organizational Change Management plan was implemented.
- Regular project reports and reviews were held.
- All major changes were made.
- The impact of all changes was measured.
- Employees were trained to operate in the new process.
- All supporting documentation, including training plans and curriculum, was released.
- A final report defining the return on investment and the impact of the future-state solution on the measurements was completed.
- The members of the BIT and the implementation teams were appropriately rewarded.

- The Organizational Change Management plan was updated to support the new process.
- The benchmarking database was updated to reflect the implemented future-state solution.

PHASE V: CONTINUOUS IMPROVEMENT

As with all improvement strategies, benchmarking needs to be a continuous effort to be effective. What is world-class today is often outmoded tomorrow. To get the most out of all the hard work that you have done in benchmarking an item, you need to make sure you have a process that will identify when there is a negative shift in the benchmark item's performance gap. The benchmark item's database must be continuously updated, and effort must be expended to continuously improve the item's performance.

Activity 19—Maintain the Benchmarking Database

Your organization has made a major investment in developing an extensive database on the benchmark item. Since it is much easier to keep the database current than to go back at a later date and try to update it, someone should be assigned to research and update the database on a continuous basis. Updates should include searches of the information available in public domain literature, internal evaluations, benchmarking partner results, and focus group activities.

As other organizations improve the performance of their benchmark item, the BIT should evaluate the potential impact on the relative performance of its benchmark item and repeat Activities 16, 17, and 18 if required. At least once a year the BIT should meet to review the status of the item.

Following is a list of the ongoing tasks conducted during Activity 19:

- A data analyst maintains the database.
- Regularly scheduled searches of public domain data are conducted, and the results are analyzed.
- The database is kept current so that it reflects the present item's performance at each internal benchmarking partner's site.
- Yearly benchmark item review meetings are conducted to identify additional action that needs to be taken to maintain the item's positive gap.

ACTIVITY 20—IMPLEMENT CONTINUOUS PERFORMANCE IMPROVEMENT

Once the future-state solution is implemented and operating effectively, the benchmarking implementation team can be dissolved and the continuous performance improvement of the item turned over to the functions that are responsible for portions or all of it. Through the use of *department improvement teams* (DITs), sometimes called *natural work teams* (NWTs), the organization should be able to improve the benchmark item's performance at an annual rate of 5 to 20 percent. During this activity, great care should be taken not to degrade the benchmark item's overall performance by making improvements that benefit one part of the item's performance while having a negative impact on another part (suboptimization).

Following is a list of the tasks completed during Activity 20:

- Department improvement teams (DITs) were formed.

- Each DIT developed a set of effectiveness and efficiency measurements related to its part of the item.

- Improvement requirements and targets were established.

- A series of improvement plans was developed and implemented by each DIT.

- The DITs were trained in team and problem-solving skills.

- The item's performance began to improve at a rate of 5 to 20 percent a year.

FLOWCHARTING AND SIMULATION MODELING TOOLS

Throughout the benchmarking process, flowcharting and simulation modeling play a very important role. Certanly flowcharts can be drawn by hand, and usually are to start with. But once the BIT has a picture of the item roughly defined, it is recomended that the BIT input this data into a computer program that can be used to calculate key measurements such as cost, cycle time, and first-time yield. The simulation modeling feature of the computer program is invaluable when the BIT is designing its future state solution. There are a few companies that sell programs capable of performing these activities. Two that can be recommended are Work Draw/Professional by Edge Software (P.O. Box 656, Pleasanton, CA 94566. Telephone: 510-462-0543) and ProModel by ProModel Corp. (1875 South State Street, Orem, UT 84058. Telephone: 801-223-4600).

HELPFUL HINTS FOR SUCCESSFUL BENCHMARKING

BENCHMARKING'S CRITICAL SUCCESS FACTORS

The benchmarking process has produced outstanding results in some organizations, good results in most, fair results in many, and little or no results in others. The following is a list of critical success factors that must be addressed if an organization is to have a productive benchmarking process:

1. Top management must actively lead and support the benchmarking process.
2. Benchmarking must be defined correctly. It is not just comparative analysis.
3. Resources must be set aside for benchmarking.
4. Projects need to be prioritized and competitive areas addressed first.
5. The organization must have a comprehensive understanding of how its item functions and performs before it approaches benchmarking partners.
6. The benchmarking process must be focused on implementing the future-state solution, not on collecting and analyzing data.

7. There must be a commitment to a continuous, ongoing benchmarking effort that makes it part of the management process, not a "flavor of the month."

8. At a minimum, all managers and key support personnel need to understand the benchmarking process.

9. Results must be measured in a way that evaluates the benchmarking effort's impact on the bottom line.

10. Benchmarking projects must apply Organizational Change Management concepts to the target areas from the beginning of a project and continually apply them after the future-state solution is implemented.

11. Benchmarking item teams must develop a specific and realistic action plan.

12. The organization must embrace change as a way of life.

13. Benchmarking projects should be embedded into each function's yearly business plans, and the improvements should be reflected in future budgets.

14. Management must select benchmarking item team (BIT) members who can implement the results of the benchmarking study.

15. Management and BIT members should be measured on how they will use the benchmarking process.

16. The organization needs to develop an attitude of questioning why it must be "invented here."

17. The organization must realize that the outside world is changing rapidly, so improvement efforts must be directed at being better than today's best.

18. Critical business processes must be identified and improved.

19. Creativity, innovativeness, and new ideas must be

required of all employees. All efforts must be encouraged. Even noble failures should be rewarded.

20. The organization must be willing to share information with internal and external benchmarking partners.

21. Each benchmarking partner must be selected carefully to make sure it is truly the best and not just an organization that presents a great story.

22. Benchmarking should be used as a way to make good items better or the best, not only as a way to correct problems or help the organization when it has its "back to the wall."

23. Benchmarking results need to be translated into return-on-investment figures.

24. The organization needs to establish a balanced scorecard measurement system early in the benchmarking process.

25. A reward-and-recognition system that reinforces desired behavior needs to be established.

26. Line management needs to accept responsibility for driving the benchmarking process at the item level. Managers should also be measured on how well they meet this responsibility.

27. The benchmarking process must focus first on industry-best practices and next on performance measurements.

28. Organizations should not accept a single benchmarking partner's approach. They should try to combine the best concepts and practices of all the benchmarking partners. This approach allows the organization's item to leapfrog the pack.

29. The benchmarking process should be applied to organizations outside the industry, as well as to competitors.

30. Benchmarks must be updated regularly, and the benchmarking process must be improved on an ongoing basis.

BENEFITS OF BENCHMARKING

When properly implemented, benchmarking is very beneficial to those organizations classified as winners and survivors. Some of the benefits are that benchmarking:

- Defines the gap between the organization's performance and other organizations' performance, creating a desire to change
- Bases goals on external consideration and known performance standards
- Integrates the best practices into the organization
- Creates goals that are more aggressive and more credible
- Leads to faster implementation of new approaches, with less risk
- Provides a better focus on external customers and consumers
- Develops effective measurement systems
- Improves individual and team creativity
- Provides many options to solve an individual problem
- Results in breakthrough improvements
- Brings together the strategic plan and the organization's improvement efforts
- Breaks down old roadblock attitudes ("We have done that before")
- Identifies strengths that the organization can build upon as well as weaknesses that need to be improved

- Has a positive impact on employee pride and morale
- Is an important enabler that helps the organization compete for the Malcolm Baldrige National Quality Award
- Provides a high return on investment
- Helps the organization become the best it can be
- Develops valuable professional contacts
- Provides an excellent picture of the future-state solution before it is implemented
- Provides more realistic implementation plans
- Builds a high degree of cooperation among different functions and individuals within the organization

CAUTION

It would be remiss to point out only the benefits of benchmarking. There are some pitfalls that all organizations must consider as well. Designing the organization's benchmarking process to consider the critical-success factors discussed above will overcome most of the potential pitfalls. Still, there are three that should be highlighted.

1. The best organizations are continuously being toppled and replaced by newcomers. For example, of the top 10 admired corporations on *Fortune* magazine's list in 1989, only 2 (Rubbermaid and 3M) made the 1995 list (see Table 7-1). Xerox, which made business process benchmarking popular in the mid-1980s, ranked 82 out of the fewer than 400 organizations included in *Fortune's* 1995 list.

If your organization copies today's best and takes a long time (18 to 30 months) to implement the future-state solution, by the time that solution is implemented it may already

TABLE 7-1   How the Best Corporations Do Over Time

CORPORATION	1989 RATING	1995 RATING
Merck	1	24
Rubbermaid	2	1
3M	3	8
Philip Morris	4	202
Wal-Mart Stores	5	52
Exxon	6	70
PepsiCo	7	72
Boeing	8	13
Herman Miller	9	25
Shell Oil	10	38

be obsolete. As a result, your organization will not achieve the required competitive advantage it is looking for. Management needs to look not only at what today's best organizations are doing, but also at what the up-and-coming organizations are doing.

2. Some organizations become concerned because even though they are benchmarking their competitors, they are not gaining a significant competitive advantage. The reason for the lack of bottom-line results is that most organizations today are improving exponentially, causing many of them to stay on a par with their competitors even though they (the organizations) are improving. As a result, their market share does not increase. An organization that is utilizing the improvement process may even be losing ground—usually because the organization has observed what its competitors

were implementing and decided to copy it. Such an organization usually starts its improvement activities 1 to 2 years behind its competitors.

Figure 7-1 shows the exponential improvement curves for two different organizations. Curve A represents the improvement curve for a leading competitor and Curve B represents the curve for a latecomer to the improvement effort. Both curves are identical, but the second curve is offset by a year. You will note that as both organizations progress, the difference between the two curves becomes greater because of the exponential nature of improvement curves.

You have just learned Improvement Rule Number 1: You cannot copy your competitors, because when you get to where you want to be, they will be far ahead of you. When you are behind, you must improve at a steeper rate than your competitors in order to be competitive.

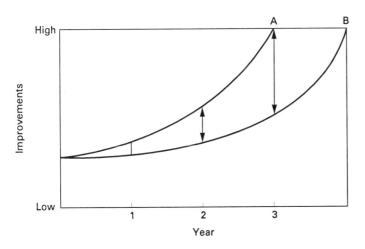

Figure 7-1. *Two identical improvement curves offset by a year.*

3. The effectiveness of the benchmarking process varies significantly depending upon the maturity level of the organization. Benchmarking can even have a negative impact on lower-performing organizations. This statement is based on *International Quality Study (IQS) Best Practices Report,* a report prepared by Ernst & Young LLP and the American Quality Foundation in 1992. This report documents the results of the world's largest and most comprehensive management practices' study. After months of pouring over more than 1.5 million inputs, using regression and correlation analysis in an effort to relate individual management practices to performance, the research team reported the following about benchmarking:

> The lower group (lower-performing organizations) actually shows a negative impact from benchmarking marketing and sales systems.

> We believe there are at least two reasons why lower-performing organizations do not benefit greatly from benchmarking practices. First, they are likely to be looking at inappropriate role models. The common practice in benchmarking is to examine the "best of the best," or world-class organizations. Yet the IQS data have shown again and again that the practices that distinguish higher-performing organizations are almost always ineffective when adopted by lower-performing organizations. Lower performers probably would find organizations that are on the threshold of medium performance, rather than world-class organizations, to be more helpful models. Second, the lower-performing organizations need to focus their resources on their core infrastructure and not diffuse their focus with the sophisticated practices they would see in the best of the best.

WHAT BENCHMARKING IS NOT

Benchmarking is an important tool in the improvement arsenal, but it is just one of more than 400 different tools that should be part of every organization's improvement toolbox.* The following list describes what benchmarking is *not*. It should not be used:

- Just to win the Malcolm Baldrige National Quality Award
- To cure all the organization's ills—many ills cannot be cured by benchmarking
- As a short-term process that will be dropped in 1 or 2 years
- To eliminate the need for creativity
- To copy another organization's product design
- To get improvements without investing resources—benchmarking is not free
- As a one-sided gathering of information
- As a way to justify headcount reductions without changing the accompanying processes
- As a form of industrial tourism
- As a training ground for new and/or inexperienced employees
- To improve items that have a negative performance gap only
- To compare organizations with their competitors only
- As a one-time comparison or improvement
- As a quick fix

---

*To understand how benchmarking fits into the organization's total improvement strategy, we recommend that you consult our book *Total Improvement Management* (McGraw-Hill, 1995).

- To improve items that can be measured only quantitatively
- To impress top management only
- To use up some idle time if there is nothing better to do with it

BENCHMARKING'S RULES OF THE ROAD

As with any process, benchmarking has specific rules that must be followed to get the best results. Designing the organization's benchmarking process and implementation strategy to ensure that it will adhere to these rules will save the organization a great deal of time and trouble. The following is a list of benchmarking's rules of the road:

1. Get top management's commitment to the benchmarking process first.
2. Design your benchmarking process before you start to benchmark.
3. Start with a few critical items.
4. Define a very specific code of ethics and be sure that everyone engaged in the benchmarking process is trained on its content and intent.
5. Train all the employees who will be actively engaged in the benchmarking process in the benchmarking methodology and the appropriate supporting tools.
6. Characterize your benchmark item first.
7. Never ask a benchmarking partner for information that you would not share with that partner. Be very careful not to obtain confidential information from your bench-

marking partner, even if you would be willing to share that information with the partner.

8. Tell your benchmarking partner up front how the data will be used.

9. Combine inputs from all your benchmarking partners to define a number of potential future-state solutions. Then select the best-value solution for implementation. This is not necessarily the one that results in the item's best performance.

10. Be satisfied not to be the best. Stop when additional cost does not improve your competitive position.

11. Start managing the benchmark item's change process the first week that the benchmarking item team is formed.

12. Do not try to collect all the data that is out there. If you do try, you will never get beyond the data collection stage.

13. Don't copy; create. Analyze what the benchmarking item team has collected so that the data can be transformed into information. Then be creative with the use of this information to design the future-state solution.

14. No organization is the best at everything it does. Find the right benchmarking partner for each item that is benchmarked.

15. Keep focused on implementation of the future-state solution. Remember, the very best plan is useless if it does not get implemented. Don't analyze the benchmarking process to death.

16. Make line managers responsible for benchmarking, and measure their performance.

17. Establish a reward-and-recognition system that supports the desired benchmarking behaviors.

MANAGEMENT'S ROLE IN THE BENCHMARKING PROCESS

The success of the benchmarking process is directly related to the importance that management places on it. No management involvement yields no results. Passive involvement yields poor results. If management only provides resources, this minimum commitment will yield fair results. If you want the best return on the organization's investment, management must be personally committed to the process. Be sure that the necessary resources are included in the annual business plans, that the organization's strategic plan reflects the benchmarking process, and that managers are willing to give freely of their time to review and talk about the benchmarking efforts. In a discussion about benchmarking, Bob Palmer, CEO of Digital Equipment Corporation, stated that DEC "fully commits to its continuous use of a method/technique/tool for a minimum of 7 years."

Top managers must fully believe that benchmarking is beneficial to the organization; they must commit themselves to being involved in the benchmarking process and align their "walk with their talk." Managers open their mouths and move their tongues to create words. Employees *listen* to the words rolling off the tongue in the manager's mouth and *wait,* but they *watch* the tongue in the manager's shoes to see if the manager truly means what he or she is saying. If the two tongues are not going in the same direction, bedlam is created and no progress is made.

The following actions and behaviors are important if management is going to champion the benchmarking process. Managers must:

• Be involved in developing the benchmarking process

- Be involved in the prioritization of the benchmarking projects
- Supply the required resources
- Include benchmarking improvements and plans in the strategic and business plans
- Track the benchmarking projects and review progress
- Spread an attitude that benchmarking will save the organization work, not create more work
- Communicate the importance of benchmarking within the organization (through meetings, letters, organization newspapers, policies, and so on) and outside the organization (by attending conferences, holding training sessions, presenting papers, writing reports, and the like).
- Reward successful benchmarking efforts
- Take appropriate corrective action when benchmarking projects fall behind schedule
- Review benchmarking project status monthly
- Ensure that benchmarking is part of the manager's measurement plan and that of appropriate employees
- Participate in at least one benchmarking project every 2 years

As Bob Palmer of Digital Equipment Corporation noted: "Results of benchmarking efforts are incorporated into the strategic planning process, strategic direction is set, and goals and performance targets are established based upon best-in-class information."

Management must help the organization move through the four attitude stages that accompany the benchmarking process.

STAGE 1: DON'T KNOW AND DON'T WANT TO KNOW. The organization is happy with things as they are. It sees no reason to do anything differently.

STAGE 2: BENCHMARKING IS POPULAR, SO LET'S DO IT. Some managers start to measure how well their organization is doing, hoping that it will be the best but not wanting to change anything. Their professional associates outside the organization are benchmarking, and it seems to be the "in" thing to do. There is a lot of interest in gathering data on how good another organization is, but little interest in understanding *why* other organizations are better. Management's corrective action takes the form of trying to justify the differences.

STAGE 3: BENCHMARKING IS GOOD FOR PRODUCTS AND SERVICES. Although many organizational functions use benchmarking to some degree to compare performance, the focus of their improvement activities is on the products and services that interface directly with the customer/consumer. In other functional areas, management feels uncomfortable and a bit defensive when negative gaps are identified. In the support areas, benchmarking is frequently directed at outside organizations that are not the best—because such an approach reflects favorably on the benchmarking manager.

STAGE 4: BENCHMARKING DIRECTLY RELATES TO THE ORGANIZATION'S GOALS AND STRATEGIC PLAN. At this point in time, benchmarking is internalized in the organization. Management at all levels has accepted benchmarking as one of the useful tools to improve their organization's performance. They have stopped being defensive about the results of the data collection phase of the benchmarking process. Management uses benchmarking data to help justify proposed changes.

C H A P T E R
E I G H T

IN CONCLUSION

If you can't meet a world standard of quality at the world's best price, you're not even in the game.   JACK WELCH
CEO of General Electric

Jack Welch makes a good point. Unfortunately, most organizations don't know what the world standards are, so they don't know how to get in the game. That is what benchmarking is all about—providing the organization with world-class standards, then helping them meet those standards so that their organization can remain competitive.

INTRODUCTION

You have traveled down a long trail leading through the maze that makes up the best practices applied to the benchmarking process. The route may seem complex and hazardous, but it is simpler to navigate than it is to describe. It is a route that many organizations have traveled with great success, and your organization can be equally successful if it follows the rules of the road listed in this book.

Most improvement efforts start by looking inward to see what problems the organization is having, then looking outward to define which customers' needs are not being met. This is an excellent approach for organizations that are in deep trouble—as Xerox, Motorola, and General Motors were in the early 1980s. It is a reactive strategy that is designed to help the organization survive. The disadvantage with the problem-solving approach to improvement is that it helps the organization meet customer requirements, not to excel. The question confronting any organization that has survived the 1980s and mid-1990s is how to get past the mediocrity of simply meeting requirements to become a winning organization that is accepted as world class. This is where benchmarking comes in. It provides the organization with the information, awareness, motivation, and knowledge that often result in major breakthroughs in organizational performance. Benchmarking provides a new understanding of what can be achieved, an understanding that internal-focused and customer-focused measurements cannot provide.

Organizations in all fields (banking, health care, automotive, high-tech, low-tech) and around the world (Australia, New Zealand, Argentina, China, South Africa), are making use of benchmarking to revolutionize their performance. The concept of benchmarking is not new. Even applying it to business processes is not new. Many published studies made by universities and businesses—reports comparing financial, stocking, and sales processes—date back to the late nineteenth century. What has made benchmarking so popular recently is that there is a great deal of information available in the public domain. In today's information-rich society, there is more information available about best practices and procedures than ever before. This knowledge base is rapidly changing, replacing present best practices with even better ones. The vast public-domain database makes it necessary to define and document the process of benchmarking so that it can be communicated and repeated.

Another key factor that has made benchmarking so popular is that benchmarking professionals have pushed hard to get the benchmarking concept deeply embedded in the Malcolm Baldrige National Quality Award. Today it is almost impossible to win the award without a very active benchmarking program that is effectively used throughout the organization. This emphasis can lead to serious problems when low-performing organizations begin to copy best-of-breed organizations. Low-performing organizations should get out of trouble before they start benchmarking world-class organizations.*

Although the criteria for the Malcolm Baldrige Award are evolving each year, at the present time benchmarking is mentioned in three different sections and impacts seven different examination items that together total 270 points. The seven items are:

Item 2.2   Competitive Comparisons and Benchmarks

Item 5.2   Analysis and Improvement of Product and Service Production and Delivery Processes

Item 5.3   Improvement of Business Processes and Support Services

Item 6.1   Quality Level Comparisons against Competitors for Key Product and Service Features

Item 6.2   Overall Performance Comparisons against Established Benchmarks

Item 6.3   Comparisons with Appropriate Benchmarking Partners for Business Processes and Support Services

Item 6.4   Comparison of Your Suppliers' Quality against Competitors and Benchmarks

Xerox started the recent enthusiasm for benchmarking when it credited it as the tool that caused the company's

---

*These findings were reported in *International Quality Study Best Practices*, prepared by Ernst & Young LLP and published by ASQC in 1992.

performance to turn around in the mid-1980s. As John Cooney, one of Xerox's marketing managers, put it, "Benchmarking has become a way of life at Xerox." But after using the benchmarking process for over 3 years, David Kearns, CEO of Xerox, discovered that the organization's best units were at least a year behind in their quality improvement schedule, and that other units were even worse off. In analyzing the problem, Kearns reported, "Half of it was because we were too aggressive on our goals and just couldn't pull them off, but the other half was because we weren't doing a better job. We were promoting people, but not necessarily quality people." To offset this problem, the employees' and managers' assessment program was tied into Xerox's quality program. As Kearns noted, "That decision had as much impact as anything we've done."

Today Xerox's improvement effort includes many other tools besides benchmarking. One of its most effective programs, known as Focused Executives, assigns top marketing executives to be the primary interface with major organizations, ensuring quick response to the customer's problems and needs. It also provides an effective way for Xerox to identify future needs. Again, not a new idea. For example, IBM took this approach a step further as early as the 1960s when it assigned each executive, independent of the organization he or she was in, a specific major customer to work with and understand.

The point of this discussion is that benchmarking is just a tool—one of the more than 400 improvement tools available to your organization today. Don't put all your eggs in the benchmarking basket. For an organization to become and stay world class, it must implement a total improvement management process that includes benchmarking as one of the tools in its toolbox.

Benchmarking is helping organizations bring on new ideas. It makes organizations reexamine the way they are doing things. When U.S. organizations dominated the world's market, they didn't have outside pressures driving their improvement efforts, so they could take their own sweet time. Today U.S. organizations cannot, because they no longer dominate the world's market, so their benchmarking activities must take on an international focus.

Don't misunderstand. The United States is not second-best in everything. In many industries, it is still the world leader. But there is a lot of competition out there, hungry to take away customers. Foreign competitors are just as creative as American organizations (for example, foreign organizations accounted for over 50 percent of new U.S. patents in 1994), and they can still remember what it is like to go hungry. In my view, there is a direct correlation between the last time a worker went hungry and his or her work ethic.

IBC, based in Houston, Texas, conducted a survey of 76 organizations and found that

- Benchmarking was considered to be a necessary tool for survival
- Most firms did not know how to systematically conduct a benchmarking project
- 95 percent of the organizations surveyed felt that most firms do not know how to benchmark
- 79 percent of the organizations believed that top management must be very actively involved if the benchmarking process is going to be successful

In a survey of 770 organizations in Europe, the Benchmarking Centre (UK) found that:

- 89 percent of the organizations rated "finding competent benchmarking partners" as their most important requirement

- 70 percent of the UK organizations were doing benchmarking
- 95 percent of the organizations were willing to share information with a benchmarking center

During World War II a recruitment poster read: "Join the Navy and see the world." Too many managers and professionals today view benchmarking in the same light. They have changed the slogan to read, "Join a benchmarking team and see the world." This is far from the truth. Studies show that for every hour spent visiting a benchmarking partner's site, over 200 hours are required in planning, collecting, and analyzing data and implementing changes. Benchmarking is not site visits. It is creative analysis of thousands of pieces of information to bring about a change in the benchmark item—a change that is often as drastic as the caterpillar's transformation into the monarch butterfly.

When all is said and done, the most difficult part of the benchmarking process is awakening to the fact that your operation does not know it all. Most U.S. organizations are just too egotistical to admit that they can learn anything from another organization. The benchmarking process starts when you admit that your counterparts in mainland China, Portugal, Malaysia, Sweden, the United Kingdom, France, and elsewhere may have an idea that is better than yours.

WHAT CAN BE ACCOMPLISHED BY USING BENCHMARKING?

Hundreds, if not thousands, of organizations have used benchmarking as an effective way to improve their performance. The following are some well-known examples of what can be accomplished.

Eastman Kodak

In 1991, The Kodak Park Division benchmarked its control over air emission of organic solvents in an effort to reduce methylene chloride. In a 4-year period, it was able to reduce the methylene chloride air emission levels from 8.9 to 4.6 million pounds a year—an improvement of approximately 50 percent.

Eastman Kodak identified Motorola as being world-class at closing month-end accounting records. At the time (1991), it was taking Kodak 20 days after its end-of-the-month date to close its books; Motorola was doing it in 2 days. After some discussion with Motorola's finance organization and a site visit, Kodak developed a future-state solution that brought about significant improvement in its operations. Here are some of the key changes that were made:

- Standard reporting formats were used, so that all units reported in the same way.
- Information was transferred by floppy disks or by telephone lines.
- A computer program was developed that consolidated and analyzed the many inputs from different organizations and locations.
- The old 28-day accounting month was dropped in favor of a calendar month. This eliminated one accounting period each year.

Digital Equipment

Digital Equipment Corporation's benchmarking efforts in the 1980s allowed it to become one of the best-in-class operations. Its work in electronic funds transfer, direct deposit, and standardization has made it the organization to benchmark for many payroll departments throughout the world. As a result of implementing its future-state solution DEC has:

- One of the lowest cost-per-person payroll systems in the United States
- An outstanding record for the accuracy and timeliness of its direct-deposit process
- The highest volunteer participation of all major U.S. organizations in direct-deposited checks
- Extensively streamlined and automated its payroll processes
- Decreased payroll processing costs by 50 percent
- Reduced the headcount required to process payroll by 50 percent
- Reduced cycle time to process payroll by 67 percent

DEC benchmarked its manufacturing operations and found that its costs were too high by 30 to 40 percent. This knowledge heightened the priorities set on benchmarking. Today, benchmarking efforts have been initiated in all segments of the business. DEC is engaged not only in process benchmarking, but also in product benchmarking. The company uses what it calls "competitive analysis/teardown" (reverse engineering) throughout the organization. Some typical benchmarking results follow:

- New product development cycle time for a drive product fell from 30 months to 12 months.
- The cost to qualify new components was reduced by 50 percent.
- New product development costs decreased by 25 percent.
- Benchmarking identified over $300 million in improvement opportunities in power manufacturing plant operations and module processes alone.

- Benchmarking property management processes resulted in the elimination of over 50 buildings and an added reduction of 12.7 percent in costs related to the remaining buildings. Density was improved by 34.5 percent.

- Over a 1-year period, one materials function (storage group) reported a 30 percent improvement in inventory turns, a 25 percent reduction in cycle time, and a 15 percent reduction in material costs. In addition, productivity in the group went up by 25 percent.

XEROX

Probably the most famous, or at least one of the most famous, benchmarking studies was conducted in 1982, when Xerox compared its logistics and distribution process to the same process at L. L. Bean, a mail-order clothing distributor in Maine. Of the 10 percent productivity improvement in the Xerox warehousing operation, 3 to 5 percent was directly attributed to benchmarking with L. L. Bean.

In 1989, Xerox benchmarked its inventory practices and found that among its 13 benchmarking partners, Singer was the best, with inventory costs running at 11.4 percent of sales. Another benchmarking partner's inventory was running at 25 percent of sales. Xerox's was running at about 19 percent. By focusing on business processes and manufacturing processes, Xerox was able to reduce inventory as a percentage of sales to less than 12 percent in the following 5 years. The result was a reduction in inventory value from $400 million to $150 million.

OTHER EXAMPLES

A major computer hardware manufacturer benchmarked its supplier processes with organizations like Motorola, Xerox, and Ford. As a result, in 8 months the manufacturer was able to:

- Cut the supplier base by 50 percent
- Reduce defective products received at its plants by 25 percent
- Increase on-time delivery rates to almost 95 percent

Ritz-Carlton in Dearborn, Michigan, benchmarked housekeeping activities and discovered that one of its competitor's hotels in New York City was using a 4-person cleaning team. As it turned out, Ritz-Carlton's site in Maui, Hawaii, was using cleaning teams as well. As a result, the hotel implemented the team-cleaning concept, with the following improvements:

- Cleaning cycle time down 65 percent
- Defect levels down 42 percent
- Improved safety for guests and staff (fewer unlocked rooms)
- Productivity up over 15 percent per employee
- Reduction in individual travel by 64 percent
- Reduction in guest interruptions by 33 percent (honor bar restocking done as part of cleaning)

BENCHMARKING AWARDS

Whether your organization has done benchmarking for a number of years or is just starting out, we strongly recommend that you set your sights on winning one or more of the three prestigious benchmarking awards given out by the American Productivity and Quality Center (APQC) each year:

- Award for Excellence in Benchmarking
- Benchmarking Research Prize
- Benchmarking Study Prize

AWARD FOR EXCELLENCE IN BENCHMARKING

The Award for Excellence in Benchmarking recognizes organizations that have consistently applied benchmarking concepts throughout their operation and have been effective in applying such concepts to both strategic and tactical business processes. A maximum of three awards will be presented each year in the small and large business categories. The guidelines used in evaluating applicants for the award have been well defined and published by the American Productivity and Quality Center. These guidelines also provide an excellent self-assessment tool for an organization beginning or involved in the benchmarking process. Table 8-1 lists the categories and subcategories related to the Award for Excellence in Benchmarking.

TABLE 8-1   Categories Related to the Award for Excellence in Benchmarking

NAME	POINTS
Category 1: Strategic Planning Integration and Information Structure	
1.A—Strategic Planning Integration	170
1.B—Information Structure	60
Category 2: Benchmarking Process and Support Structure	
2.A—Benchmarking Process	150
2.B—Support Structure	80
Category 3: Teamwork and Employee Involvement	140
Category 4: Business Alliances and Networking	100
Category 5: Results and Improvements in Benchmarked Processes	300
Total:	1000

The recognition process is modeled after the Malcolm Baldrige National Quality Award. Candidates submit a written application in keeping with predefined guidelines (35 pages maximum). The applications are scored by examiners. Those applications classified as "best practices" are reviewed by a panel of judges to determine if a site visit will be made. Finalists receive a site visit to verify and clarify information contained in the written application. Formal winners are selected on the basis of these site visits.

Awards are presented in two categories:

- Small organizations—independent business entities with fewer than 500 full-time-equivalent employees
- Large organizations—business entities with more than 500 full-time-equivalent employees

INDIVIDUAL AND TEAM BENCHMARKING AWARDS

The two other APQC awards are designed to recognize individuals and teams for their outstanding contributions to the benchmarking process.

BENCHMARKING RESEARCH AWARD.   The research award is conferred for the development of technical aspects of benchmarking. It encourages original contributions in data collection and analysis and in integration of benchmarking techniques. It also encourages the creative use of statistical and managerial techniques to advance the benchmarking methodology. The award has two categories: academic research and applied research. No more than two awards per category are given out each year. The application is limited to 20 pages and should address the following:

- Creativity and innovation (200 points)

- Technical sophistication (200 points)
- Demonstrated or potential applicability (200 points)
- Practicality (200 points)
- Portability (200 points)

BENCHMARKING STUDY AWARD.   The study award is given to benchmarking item teams to promote excellence in the way benchmarking studies are undertaken. The award can be given to a maximum of five recipients per year. The application is limited to 20 pages and should cover the following:

- Planning the study (100 points)
- Collecting information (50 points)
- Analyzing data (50 points)
- Results and improvements (100 points)

GENERAL INFORMATION ABOUT THE AWARDS

For each award, there are three possible levels of recognition:

Gold	Model of Excellence
Silver	Outstanding Achievement
Bronze	Distinguished Achievement

For individuals, teams, and organizations interested in applying for these awards, a notice of intent should be filed with the American Productivity and Quality Center by early September. The final applications should be delivered by early December. The awards are usually presented at a conference in June of the following year. The application fees listed below are based on 1994 benchmarking award guidelines. The fee schedule may be revised each year.*

- Award for Excellence in Benchmarking—$900 for large businesses; $450 for small businesses
- Benchmarking Study Award—$300
- Benchmarking Research Award—$150

ORGANIZATIONAL CHANGE MANAGEMENT

It would be remiss to close this book without once again emphasizing the importance of using the Organizational Change Management methodology in conjunction with the benchmarking process. Benchmarking is a truly effective way to introduce changes that have a very high potential for improving an organization's performance. However, performance improvement has three ingredients:

- Technology
- Process
- People

Benchmarking is effective in identifying the best technologies and best practices. Unfortunately, it is not designed to address the people side of the equation. All too often, an

---

*For more information on benchmarking awards, contact the American Productivity and Quality Center, International Benchmarking Clearinghouse, 123 North Post Oak Lane, Houston, TX 77024. Telephone 800-776-9676. Fax 713-681-3705. Ask for a copy of the most recent benchmarking award guidelines.

outstanding future-state solution, when implemented, produces only fair results—because the people who are impacted and have to change do not embrace the solution and sometimes even sabotage it. Change is a process. It must be managed like any other process to get satisfactory results.

Too often no one considers the people who will have to change until the future-state solution has been defined and approved. The change process should start as soon as the BIT is assigned and must continue long after the change is fully implemented. By the time the future-state solution is defined, the sustaining sponsors and advocates should have been well trained and should understand their roles in support of the future-state solution. In addition, the individuals who must change (targets) should already understand the pain related to the present state.

The benchmarking implementation team is usually technically very competent—but technical expertise is only half the job that a change agent must master. Technical excellence gets the change implemented. It will not make it operational. Forced change is always resisted and seldom effective. It is absolutely mandatory that the BIT and the implementation team be trained to utilize the Organizational Change Management methodology, because that methodology can be as important as the benchmarking process itself.*

The basic philosophy, spirit, and drive of an organization have far more to do with its relative achievement than do technological or economic resources, organizational structures, innovation, and timing. All these things weigh heavily in success. But they are, I think, transcended by how

---

*For more information on Organizational Change Management, read our book entitled *Total Improvement Management* (McGraw-Hill, 1995).

strongly the people in the organization believe in its basic precepts and how faithfully they carry them out.

THOMAS J. WATSON, JR.
Past President and Chairman of the
Board, IBM Corporation

SUMMARY

Improvement is key to survival for today's businesses. If you are not improving, you are losing ground. The best organizations are the ones that have continuous improvement built into their corporate cultures. Benchmarking provides a way to judge how well your organization is performing compared with the "best of breed" and identifies how the best got to be the best.

Every time your organization's name, products, services, or people come in contact with customers or potential customers, the organization is evaluated and scored. To remain competitive, you must make sure that the evaluation places you in the "big leagues," with the rest of the best organizations.

Benchmarking must go beyond just product processes, and justify all business activities, because it will not be long before all organizations provide high-quality products. Product quality will be a given. Competitive advantage will then come from the excellence of all your customer interfaces, and the demonstrated pride your people have in their organization.

Benchmarking is not a new process. It has been used in organizations around the world for years to study competitive products. In recent years the benchmarking process has been refined and has become an even more valuable tool on the organization's "improvement workbench." Benchmarking is particularly valuable because it:

- Enables an organization to set challenging, yet realistic, targets
- Provides a process for improvement
- Facilitates prediction of future trends
- Helps an organization learn from the very best, so that it can be more competitive
- Provides information on how to improve

Has benchmarking been successful? Just listen to what Edward Tracy, operations vice president for AT&T's MMS Division, had to say on the subject: "Not just mildly successful but enormously successful. What this process enables us to do is to identify voids. It's a structured discipline for analyzing a process to find improvement opportunities. Just 12 months ago I was skeptical. But, when I saw it in action, I realized the benefits of the process."

Systematic benchmarking can enable your organization to be the very best. Without it, you will never truly know how good you are, how good you should be, or how to become the best you can be. Isn't it time you really understood the full potential of your organization?

I believe the real difference between success and failure in a corporation can very often be traced to the question of how well the organization brings out the greatest energies and talents of its people. What does it do to help those people find common cause and sense of direction through the many changes which take place from one generation to another?   THOMAS J. WATSON, JR.
*Past President and Chairman of the
Board, IBM Corporation*

FREE BENCHMARKING CLEARINGHOUSE

Communications technologies have also assisted in reducing the task of finding and obtaining relevant data from a suitable benchmarking partner. Through the Internet, Ernst & Young LLP SYSTEMCORP Inc. is now providing Benchmarx, a database of current and relevant benchmarking fields and other pertinent information from world-class organizations. The site is actively updated by experts, and is one of the most cost-effective ways to benchmark. Until January 1, 1997, it is accessible to all who have purchased this book free of charge when they submit their data from one benchmarking project. You may reach their Web site at:

HTTP://WWW.SYSTEMCORP.COM/BENCHMARX

SUGGESTED READING AND INFORMATION SOURCES

BOOKS AND BROCHURES

American Productivity and Quality Center, 1993. *Benchmarking the Best*, Houston, Tex.

American Productivity and Quality Center, 1993. *The Benchmarking Management Guide*, Houston, Tex.

American Productivity and Quality Center, 1993. *Tools and Techniques for Effective Benchmarking Studies*, Houston, Tex.

Balm, Gerald J., 1992. *Benchmarking: A Practitioner's Guide for Becoming and Staying the Best of the Best*, QPMA Press, Schaumburg, Ill.

Benchmarking for Process Improvement, 1994. Xerox Quality Solutions, Rochester, N.Y.

Bendell, Tony, Louise Boulter, and John Kelly, 1993. *Benchmarking for Competitive Advantage*, McGraw-Hill, New York.

Bogan, Christopher E. and Michael J. English, 1994. *Benchmarking for Best Practices*, McGraw-Hill, New York.

Bosomworth, Charles E., 1993. *The Executive Benchmarking Guidebook*. The Management Roundtable, Boston.

Camp, Robert C., 1989. *Benchmarking: The Search for Industry Best Practices That Lead to Superior Performance*. ASQC Quality Press, Milwaukee, Wisc.

Camp, Robert C., 1995. *Business Process Benchmarking*. ASQC Quality Press, Milwaukee, Wisc.

Caropreso, Frank, (ed.), 1990. "Competitive Benchmarking: Xerox's Powerful Quality Tool." In *Making Total Quality Happen*, Research Report No. 937, The Conference Board, New York.

Christopher, William F., and Carl G. Thor, 1993. *Handbook for Productivity Measurement and Improvement*. Edited by Productivity Press, Portland, Oreg.

Churchill, Gilbert A., Jr., 1983. *Marketing Research: Methodological Foundations*. 3d ed., The Dryden Press, Fort Worth, Tex.

Codling, Sylvia, 1992. *Best Practices Benchmarking: The Management Guide to Successful Implementation*. Industrial Newsletter Ltd., Bedford, U.K.

Czarnecki, Mark T., 1993. *Benchmarking Strategies in Accounting and Finance*. American Institute of Certified Public Accountants, Jersey City, N.J.

Fuld, Leonard M., 1985. *Competitor Intelligence: How to Get It— How to Use It*. Wiley, New York.

Fuld, Leonard M., 1988. *Monitoring The Competition: Find Out What's Really Going On Over There*. Wiley, New York.

Furey, Timothy R., Robert M. Fifer, Lawrence S. Pryor, and Jeffrey P. Rumberg, 1988. *Beating The Competition: A Practical Guide to Benchmarking*. Kaiser Associates, Vienna, Va.

Haim, Alexander (ed.), 1992. *Closing the Quality Gap: Lessons Learned from America's Leading Companies*. Prentice Hall, Englewood Cliffs, N.J.

Harrington, H. James, 1972. *Process Compatibility*. IBM, San Jose, Calif.

Harrington, H. James, 1991. *Business Process Improvement*. McGraw-Hill and ASQC Quality Press, New York.

Harrington, H. James, 1996. *The Complete Benchmarking Implementation Guide*, McGraw-Hill, New York.

Harrington, H. James, 1995, *Total Improvement Management*, McGraw-Hill, New York.

Harris Bank, 1992. *Conversations for the 90s: The Search for Superior Performance*, Chicago.

Hooper, John A., 1992. *Borrowing from the Best: How to Benchmark World-Class People Practices.* HR Effectiveness, Beaverton, Oreg.

Hou, Wee Chow, L. K. Sheang, and B. W. Hidajat, 1991. *Sun Tzu: War and Management, Application to Strategic Management and Thinking.* Addison-Wesley, Reading, Mass.

International Benchmarking Clearinghouse, 1992. *Planning, Organizing, and Managing Benchmarking Activities: A User's Guide.* Houston, Tex.

Jacobsen, Gary, and John Hilkirk, 1986. *Xerox: American Samurai.* Macmillan Publishing, New York.

Juran, J. M., 1989. *Juran on Leadership for Quality: An Executive Handbook.* The Free Press, New York.

Karlof, Bengt, and Svante Ostblom, 1993. *Benchmarking: Vagvisare Till Masterkap i Productivetet Och Kvalitet (Benchmarking: A Guide to Productivity and Quality Championship).* Svenska Dagbladet Förlags AB, Borjå, Finland.

Kearns, David T., and David A Nadler, 1992. *Prophets in the Dark: How Xerox Reinvented Itself and Beat Back the Japanese.* Harper Business, New York.

Leibfried, Kathleen, and Carol J. McNair, 1992. *Benchmarking: A Tool for Continuous Improvement.* Harper Business, New York.

Miller, Jeffrey, Arnoud DeMeyer, Jinichiro Nakane, and Kasra Ferdows, 1992. *Benchmarking Global Manufacturing.* Business One Irwin, Homewood, Ill.

Palermo, Richard C. (ed.), 1993. *A World of Quality: The Timeless Passport.* ASQC Quality Press, Milwaukee, Wis.

Porter, Michael E., 1980. *Competitive Strategy.* The Free Press, New York.

Prentice-Hall, 1994. *Almanac of Business and Industrial Financial Ratios,* Englewood Cliffs, N.J.

Russell, J.P., 1991. *Quality Management Benchmark Assessment.* ASQC Quality Press, Milwaukee, Wisc.

Saaty, Thomas L., 1988. *Decision-Making for Leaders: The Analytical Hierarchy Process for Decisions in a Complex World.* RWS Publications, Pittsburgh, Pa.

Sammon, William L., Mark A. Kirkland, and Robert Spitalnic, 1984. *Business Competitor Intelligence: Methods for Collecting, Organizing, and Using Information*. Wiley, New York.

Spendolini, Michael J., 1992. *The Benchmarking Book*. AMACOM Press, New York.

Sun Tzu, 1983. *The Art of War*, James Clavel (ed.). Delacorte Press, New York.

Thomas, Philip R., 1990. *Competitiveness Through Total Cycle Time: An Overview for CEOs*. McGraw-Hill, New York.

Troy, Kathryn, 1992. *Baldrige Winners on World-Class*. The Conference Board, Inc., New York.

Tyson, Kirk W. M., 1986. *Business Intelligence—Putting It All Together*. Leading Edge Publishing, Lombard, Ill.

The Verity Consulting Group, 1991. *Benchmarking*. Verity Press, Los Angeles.

Watson, Gregory H., 1992. *The Benchmarking Workbook: Adapting Best Practices for Performance Improvement*. Productivity Press, Portland, Oreg.

Watson, Gregory H., 1993. *Strategic Benchmarking: How to Rate Your Company's Performance Against the World's Best*. Wiley, New York.

Xerox Corporation Booklet, 1987. *Competitive Benchmarking: What It Is and What It Can Do for You*, Webster, N.Y.

Xerox Corporation Booklet, 1987. *Leadership Through Quality: Implementing Competitive Benchmarking, Employee Involvement and Recognition—Part I*, Webster, N.Y.

Xerox Corporation Booklet, 1988. *Competitive Benchmarking: The Path to a Leadership Position*, Webster, N.Y.

Zairi, Dr. Mohamed, 1992. *Competitive Benchmarking—An Executive Guide*. Technical Communications (Publishing) Ltd., Letchworth, U.K.

Zairi, Dr. Mohamed, and Paul Leonard, 1994. *Practical Benchmarking: The Complete Guide*. Chapman and Hall, New York.

COMPUTER TRAINING PROGRAMS AND VIDEOTAPES

Benchmarking: Competing through Quality with David Garvin and an Interview of John Kelsch from Xerox. Harvard videotape series. Nathan/Tyler, Boston, 1991.

Benchmarking Manufacturing Processes. Videotape series. Society of Manufacturing Engineers, Dearborn, Mich., 1994.

Benchmarking with Dr. H. James Harrington. Interactive software program. Learnerfirst, Birmingham, Ala., 1993.

Getting Started in the Benchmarking Process, Effective Benchmarking, and Integrating Benchmarking Data into the Strategic Process. Videotape series. Encyclopedia Britannica Educational Corporation, Chicago, 1992.

In Business: How to Steal the Best Ideas in the World. Audiocassette. London: BBC Radio 4, September 22, 1993.

INDEX